Praise for *Waiting for Dawn*

"In *Waiting for Dawn*, Marisa Renee Lee provides much-needed and gentle guidance in a world so often overrun by confusion and disruptions. With her calm and reassuring guidance, uncertainty seems a little less present and hope flourishes. It's a book that sticks with you, one you'll wish you always had on you."
—Alua Arthur, *New York Times* bestselling author of *Briefly Perfectly Human*

"Anyone will benefit from reading this amazing book! I found myself instantly uplifted by Marisa's wisdom and beautiful prose."
—Emily Oster, *New York Times* bestselling author of *Expecting Better*

"A wonderful and healing experience. I laughed and cried a bit more than I thought I would but felt reassured and comforted by her sage advice and measured approach to dealing with life's constant battles. She reminds you that the toughest times can be life changing in the best ways as well."
—Reshma Saujani, *New York Times* bestselling author of *Girls Who Code* and *Brave, Not Perfect*

Praise for *Grief Is Love*

"It's hard to fathom how much better the world would be if every grieving person had a friend like Marisa Renee Lee."
—*Glamour*

"Lee is refreshingly direct. [She] made me feel less alone in the world and, well, a little less melancholic."
—*Vulture*

"*Grief Is Love* is the closest many of us will get to understanding eternal love for another."
—Elaine Welteroth, *New York Times* bestselling author of *More Than Enough*

"*Grief Is Love* is what the world needs. Marisa's vulnerability humanizes pain, longing, and loss."
—Alexandra Elle, *New York Times* bestselling author of *How We Heal*

"If you're struggling with loss, reading this book might just be a jolt of hope."
—Adam Grant, #1 *New York Times* bestselling author of *Think Again* and *Option B*

"This book, like its author, radiates empathy, rejects platitudes, and uplifts even while interrogating life's darkest crevices."
—Alicia Menendez, MSNBC anchor and author of *The Likeability Trap*

WAITING FOR DAWN

WAITING FOR DAWN

LIVING WITH UNCERTAINTY

MARISA RENEE LEE

LEGACY
LIT

New York   Boston

Copyright © 2026 by Beacon Advisors Inc.

Cover design and illustration by Holly Ovenden
Cover copyright © 2026 by Hachette Book Group, Inc.

Hachette Book Group supports the right to free expression and the value of copyright. The purpose of copyright is to encourage writers and artists to produce the creative works that enrich our culture.

The scanning, uploading, and distribution of this book without permission is a theft of the author's intellectual property. If you would like permission to use material from the book (other than for review purposes), please contact permissions@hbgusa.com. Thank you for your support of the author's rights.

Legacy Lit
Hachette Book Group
1290 Avenue of the Americas
New York, NY 10104
HachetteBookGroup.com
@LegacyLitBooks

First edition: April 2026

Legacy Lit is an imprint of Grand Central Publishing. The Legacy Lit name and logo are registered trademarks of Hachette Book Group, Inc.

The publisher is not responsible for websites (or their content) that are not owned by the publisher.

The Hachette Speakers Bureau provides a wide range of authors for speaking events. To find out more, go to hachettespeakersbureau.com or email HachetteSpeakers@hbgusa.com.

Legacy Lit books may be purchased in bulk for business, educational, or promotional use. For information, please contact your local bookseller or the Hachette Book Group Special Markets Department at special.markets@hbgusa.com.

Print book interior design by Marie Mundaca

Library of Congress Cataloging-in-Publication Data has been applied for.

ISBNs: 9781538770191 (hardcover), 9781538770214 (ebook)

Printed in the United States of America

LSC-C

Printing 1, 2026

For Matthew, there is no one else I'd rather navigate uncertainty alongside. May we always love like the sun.

Du noir naît la lumière
"From black is born the light"

Contents

Introduction — xiii

CHAPTER 1: ...BAD — 1

CHAPTER 2: GRAY... — 11

CHAPTER 3: ...PAIN — 23

CHAPTER 4: MARATHON... — 37

CHAPTER 5: ...CONNECTION — 53

CHAPTER 6: LIGHT... — 71

CHAPTER 7: ...LOVE — 89

CHAPTER 8: FLAKE... — 103

CONTENTS

CHAPTER 9: ... HELP   115

CHAPTER 10: PERFORM ...   131

CHAPTER 11: ... HEAL   145

CHAPTER 12: HOPE ...   157

Acknowledgments   *163*

Bibliography   *169*

Introduction

You must find a way to live well today when all you want is tomorrow.

I was raised in the Black church where they are fond of saying, "You can mourn for a night, but joy, joy comes in the morning." I used to sit in a frilly church dress, hair in pigtails, lace-topped socks stuffed into Mary Janes, listening enraptured to that booming Black preacher shout down at us from the pulpit. As a child, it made me feel as though patience is enough to survive hard times: as an adult I know it is much more complex. When the darkness of uncertainty consumes our lives and we find ourselves lost in a fog of unrelenting and unexpected pain, stress, grief, or turmoil, waiting for the proverbial morning can feel like an impossible mission. Whether it is a period of financial uncertainty, a marital challenge, caretaking responsibilities, or a

INTRODUCTION

serious illness, uncertainty is coming for all of us and when it does, it is human nature to simply want it to be over. To hide, or hibernate, or distract yourself instead of dealing with whatever painful change has arisen in your life.

It can feel like everything is wrong. As if *you* must be doing something wrong for life to have turned so sideways. It is truly terrifying when you don't know if or when you're going to lose your job as a result of your company restructuring. It is absolutely destabilizing when your partner of ten years decides it is time for a change and that change does not include you. You feel emotionally excavated and something beyond overwhelmed when an unexpected ALS diagnosis enters your family. Uncertainty is real, it is hard, and it is normal, so we must find a way to live well when it enters our life.

For me, it was two years of darkness that resembled the blackest of night skies. After finally becoming parents following years of struggle and publishing a best-selling book, I expected to just ride off into the sunset on a wave of joy. Instead, my mother-in-law fell ill, and we fell into a season of anticipatory grief. During her illness, my cousin went missing and would later be found dead. Our grief and pain were tremendous and just when it seemed the dust was starting to settle and our season of uncertainty was coming to a close, I found myself sick with a debilitating illness. It

INTRODUCTION

felt like my life was impossibly hard, officially off track as well, and I had no clarity for how I was supposed to live in the midst of such physical pain and chaos. I was lonely, I was angry, I was frustrated, and most of all I was afraid. I was afraid of not getting my health back. I was afraid of losing my business. I was afraid of the impact all this stress and uncertainty was having on my marriage and my son. There was no game plan or script or strategy I could deploy to work my way out of this. I was lost in this dark forest of uncertainty with no discernable way out, forward, or through.

I didn't know what to do, or where to turn, or how to even help myself. We are often made to feel as if it is abnormal to encounter hardship in any form, be it permanent or temporary. We manage the loneliness and isolation by convincing others, and at times, ourselves as well, that we are *fine*. The current crisis is not that big of a deal, and it will surely blow over soon. When I was in my twenties and my mother was dying, the hardest question for me to answer was "How are you doing?" I couldn't answer because I did not know. I did not pause to find an answer, and the idea of simply accepting "I don't know" felt wrong.

I had no sense of how to cope or how normal it was to feel so very lost. We don't talk about these periods and how hard they are, because we are simply expected to get on with the business of living. Workplaces don't offer accommodations when your

INTRODUCTION

life has been turned upside down by divorce. There is no meaningful structural or systemic support when your mother or father suddenly falls ill and needs additional care. And when that does indeed happen, there is no playbook for how to show up for them, for everyone else in the house who has been affected, or for yourself. Oftentimes it feels as if we are simply left to catch ourselves when life suddenly falls apart.

There is no magic bullet or precise recipe for how to make your life more manageable when you're dealing with something difficult; there is no special escape hatch for emerging unscathed on the other side. But I hope this book can provide you with a bit of light when darkness descends. A softly lit candle to help guide you on your journey. No one can tell you exactly how to handle uncertainty when it arises in your life, but I hope these words, my experiences, and of course my mistakes, help you light your own way.

Moving through uncertainty with grace and compassion involves quite a bit of work, but it can be done. Nothing about it is easy because whatever you are going through isn't easy, but hard times are simply a part of life, and I think we all want to know how to do them well.

I hope your periods of uncertainty are shorter and less painful than my own, but whatever you are going through, it is going to impact you greatly and you have to find your own unique way through the

INTRODUCTION

darkness, the heaviness, the fog that has consumed your life. You must listen to your gut, be patient and gentle with yourself, and do whatever you need to do to survive transformed, but whole.

And I will not, ever, urge you to make meaning out of your pain. I will not diminish your experience by promising you it has a purpose. Uncertainty and loss and pain are all difficult and hard to live with. But what I will say is this: Anytime we are forced to endure something difficult, there are things that we learn and there are opportunities for us to grow. Darkness transforms us and in that alchemical process there is beauty and there is hope.

Whether it is the dark of night, the unlit womb that we have no memory of, or the peaceful cocoon caterpillars build for themselves to transform into butterflies, darkness is required for things to grow, for things to transform. The beauty of transformation often begins with the darkness of pain and uncertainty.

If you're in the thick of it right now, please remember that growth is almost always painful, but it never stays dark forever.

Love,

Marisa

1

...Bad

"You can't cook bacon anymore," my husband Matt said. My immediate internal response was, *What a dick*, but I quickly pivoted because he was right. He was standing by the stove in our kitchen, staring disgustedly at a cookie sheet full of bacon I'd just removed from the oven. Matt does not hide his feelings, so when I say *disgustedly*, I mean he was revolted, shocked, and appalled at what was happening in our kitchen.

I could not cook bacon anymore. *When did I become someone who made bad bacon?* I thought. *I have been an excellent cook since childhood and now I can't make bacon?* I could literally make the stuff without thinking before. Bacon, perfectly timed out of the oven while simultaneously whipping up blueberry pancakes from scratch, or some rich and fluffy scrambled eggs, and have everything arrive on the table hot, delicious, and at the same time, but now I can't cook the stuff. I only burn it.

On the night in question, I was making one of my favorite weeknight summer meals: BLTs, corn on the cob, and a caprese salad. The meal was filled with midsummer treats from the farmers market straight to our table: local tomatoes, lettuce grown by Matt, corn from a farm just up the road, and extra-special fresh mozzarella, made in-house at our favorite Italian deli, Rossi's. Add to that some of the best bacon in the world from Nueske's, a smokehouse based in Wisconsin, near where Matt grew up. Once you've tried Nueske's, it's hard to go back to "regular" bacon. This bacon is served at elite hotels worldwide and used by chefs across the country. It is delicious, pricey bacon, and I had just burned it.

It was not the first batch of bacon I had burned of late. I'd been fluctuating between actually burning it and risking burning the house down in the process and simply overcooking it. The perfect bacon has crispiness and some bend. Undercooked bacon is like a flaccid penis; too soft and droopy to do anything fun with. Overcooked bacon is like salty bits of sand; it crumbles on contact and you can't actually chew it, it just dissolves. Bacon cooked properly should be smoky, salty, and a balanced mix of crispy bits and meaningful chew. Unfortunately, my bacon was burnt. As a Black woman whose family is originally from the American South, I have been making bacon since I was eight years old, and suddenly at forty-one, a fire was about to combust in our home because I'd kept it in the oven too long. As a seasoned home cook, I was confused and, like my husband, disgusted.

I was burning bacon because my brain was no longer mine. It was not the brain I'd been accustomed to my entire life. It was not the brain that had learned how to read before kindergarten. It was not the brain that got me through taking the SATs in middle school, various gifted and talented programs, and, ultimately, into Harvard. It was not the brain that got me hired on Wall Street with zero finance experience, or the one that allowed me to write my first book while juggling a newborn on my lap. My mind was no longer mine, it was broken, and I didn't fully recognize just how broken, until Matt pointed out that I could no longer cook bacon.

The internal "chef" clock, the instincts I relied on, had been turned off and there was nothing I could do about it. Matt said to me, "It happens." I understood bacon burns. No one is perfect, but it didn't happen to *me*.

When people talk about the neurological side effects of bodily illnesses, they don't talk enough about how our minds, our brains, and how they work are affected. We don't talk about the impact of illness on the loss of our identities.

Many days I could still write. I could still work. I could still parent, but due to my long Covid, I was a different person from who I knew myself to be. My brain fog and my pain made my mind slow. Painfully slow. I had been a quick processor all my life and now it took an agonizingly long time to make connections and organize information. Information would show up and then vanish quickly. I could be in the middle of doing something and literally forget why I was there. Or, I'd say to you, "I have three things to tell you," and in the middle of thing one, thing two would simply disappear. This may be something that happens to other people all the time, but it did not happen to me.

The most basic forms of multitasking had become an obstacle—calling a friend while driving to pick up my kid from school; responding to a client email during a boring Zoom meeting; posting to social media while waiting in line at the grocery store. My brain couldn't handle doing two things at once. I was previously a woman who could entertain a toddler while making dinner, on a conference call with a demanding client, all at the same time, and now just doing one of those things might be a struggle. It was something beyond confusing; it was disorienting and frightening. Sometimes I was like my normal self, quickly making connections between things and designing thoughtful strategies for clients, and then other days, I was suddenly racked with anxiety and unable to remember basic tasks. It reminded me of when I got caught in a riptide and nearly drowned several years ago. There were brief moments when I felt I would be OK, then suddenly found myself pulled asunder, unable to breathe, internally churning and choking and gasping with no clear end in sight.

Losing something and not knowing when you'll get it back, the uncertainty if you'll ever obtain it—whether your health, a loved one, a job—is life-altering.

If it was what you were known for, and had come naturally to you, no matter how minor, the pain of losing it can feel like biting your tongue. It hurts when you drink something too hot, and you bite it over and over again before you remember to chew differently. There is no real respite. It's not the pain of a broken bone, or even a broken heart, but uncertainty is a reminder that there is something that needs to heal. There is something there requiring your attention. There is this *thing* that hurts that you cannot control and there is a very real fear that it won't go away.

Uncertainty puts you in a fog. You are perennially distracted by whatever has turned your life upside down. It brings about a loss of energy and ease. The amount of time spent rethinking, questioning yourself, standing in the kitchen confused because you opened the refrigerator to find sugar and as far as I know no one stores sugar in the fridge. The fog can make tasks that were once natural now uncomfortable or incredibly frustrating and anxiety inducing.

During the fog, our minds don't work the way we expect them to; it is hard to trust ourselves, and that lack of internal trust can lead to feelings of anxiety. I get angry and frustrated because I am suddenly navigating a complex body and all I want is to get shit done. This is what I am known for and what people expect of me. I deliver the best, all the time, in basically all areas of my life. I want to give my clients the best work. I want to write sentences that help myself and others heal. I want to give my husband and child the best of everything including bacon. When I cannot do it, that causes grief.

Every time I make a mistake that I never would have made under normal circumstances, I feel like an idiot. It's as if I am playing hide-and-seek with my former self, in the dark. I can't find the light because I can't find me. Loss of identity is dark and terrifying, and it obscures everything. Sneakers sent to an address we haven't lived in for years. My car door left open overnight draining the battery. Forgetting words while giving a speech. It all feels like failure, and for me it is failure.

I am forced to slow down my entire life. My mental processing is slow. My movements are slow. I am easily distracted, and my brain simply cannot hold as much as it once did. Seeing myself and the bacon reflected in Matt's eyes, I feel mad and defensive. I wanted to get in his face, but it's not actually about him, it's about me, my identity, and my deep personal attachment to my own intelligence. I don't know who I am in the absence of my former intelligence. Worse, I don't know if I'll ever get it back. And then there is part of me that hates myself. I hate myself for taking my old brain for granted and I also hate myself for being so attached to it. I don't know what to make of any of it, but I know I am lost.

In your life, your identity, how you define yourself, is meant to shift and change. We become graduates, parents, and spouses. We change careers, and we change as people. We grow, we evolve, and we hopefully improve over time. This is all normal and expected. What is hard is when your identity shifts or changes for reasons outside of your control. The loss of a spouse through death or divorce, the loss of a job, the loss of your good health. It is bound to happen to all of us, and in a culture that loves to preach about quick fixes, solving problems, and pulling ourselves up by our bootstraps there isn't a lot of room for the ongoing, life-altering events that will take place in many of our lives. We are made to feel weak, and we often suffer alone.

It felt like I was losing myself. I still had the essence of who I was, or at least who I've always known myself to be, but navigating the fog of uncertainty can feel like losing a vital part of your identity. When we describe ourselves, we use facts and not feelings (e.g., business owner, writer, mother). Essence is who we are at our core. It is how we feel without words and how we make others feel. Essence is the words people will use to describe you at your funeral. It's the stuff that really matters.

So, when you find yourself in a place where your identity has been altered or stripped away by forces outside of your control—remember, at the end of the day, no one, and nothing, can take who you are. There is no circumstance that can kill your essence.

There are immutable aspects of our identity. Good and bad, there are things about us that no one and nothing can erase or change. No matter what happens in this life, I will always be Lisa's daughter. My mother has been deceased for nearly twenty years, and yet there is nothing, not even death, strong enough to sever our tie. I will always be Bennett's mom. These are essential and immutable states of my being. I will also probably always be someone who tries to do too much. Who friends will describe as "extra." Who is impossibly vain, stubborn, and deeply competitive but also loyal, fierce, generous, and kind. And no matter how ill I am, I will absolutely come for you, if you come for one of my people. These things, good and bad, are all inherent to who I am, but the most important thing no one, and no life event, can take away from me, or you, are our values.

No life event can alter our core values, because that is our true essence. When you find yourself in a season of uncertainty, grief, and struggle, remember nothing can change the things that matter most about you. If you've always been hopeful, your hope matters even more in your season of suffering. If love is what you've been committed to, it will adapt to the circumstances of your life; even through loss or divorce, it will still be there. If you've always been someone who is compassionate to others, nothing can take that from you. When you feel as though you've lost control, remind yourself of who you are at your core while also being honest about your limitations today.

With my illness, I felt like my mind was no longer my own, but I needed to find a way to turn it back on. We navigate the fog well when we are able to own the ways in which we are being altered and find our own way to honor our essence and cling to the values that make us who we really are.

I had a commitment to appear on *CBS Mornings*. No way was I going to miss meeting Gayle King. I would need to rest, practice, and remove as many obstacles as possible from my path. So, I slowed down and carefully considered what I would need to be successful. I made a plan to be in the city the night before so there was no morning rush or stress on the actual day. I got deeply painful lidocaine injections to numb my head so if I was hurting, I hopefully wouldn't feel it. I outsourced my outfit selection to a neighbor and stylist, so I could focus solely on rest and my talking points. I nailed it and I had fun doing it because that is who I am. I work hard, I use my brain to help others, and I managed to find a way to make my mind work for me, on my terms amid so much uncertainty.

Sitting in the green room with Gayle King, discussing how much she enjoyed my book, reminded me that I am still Marisa. I was committed to maintaining my values while being sick and navigating the fog—of being kind, helpful, extra, and joyful. I had to be honest about and identify the things that I needed to be me. I was not able to be fast paced, process information quickly, or move my body the way I was accustomed to, and I was still living in pain. My life is different. I move more slowly to produce the same quality of work. I need to rest multiple times a day in order to be present with my son after school. I often cannot return calls from friends because it takes too much energy. I'm not myself in the traditional sense. I know parts of me and my personality have been lost to this illness and there may be parts of me that are lost forever. For now, as you wait for the fog to clear, that has to be OK...for me and you.

2

Gray...

GRAY GRIEF IS murky and uncertain like the sky before a storm officially announces itself. Nothing is black and white anymore. Everything feels heavy and dark when all you want is sunshine and blue skies and levity. Things you previously took for granted suddenly become overwhelming or virtually impossible. Being able to move your body with ease, making a dish without feeling the loss of a loved one, taking your kid to the park but instead you must work to keep the lights on. You sit somewhere in the middle of being capable and being defeated. In the gray or in between, it is neither light nor dark, and never straightforward. Yet, your grief is rooted in love. Love for the healthy version of yourself, love for when life was straightforward and routine, love for the person, pet, or job that is no longer in your life. Previously, you went to work, made dinner, walked your dog, and maintained the same routine the next day; now you have no idea what tomorrow may bring, but it will probably involve some degree of pain.

When we are no longer able to fully access a self that we recognize, can't access the activities we love, or the people we love, and the things that make us who we are due to some uncertain event, it causes deep pain. It is this pain that feels like an open wound, because in uncertainty there is no closure. Healing may arrive one day, but not today.

This Gray Grief can feel like it's blown up your life. You are navigating the rubble of a once neat and tidy existence. Oftentimes in Gray Grief it doesn't show up as clearly as a sickness or loss of a loved one; you may not even know what you are navigating through. It could take weeks or months to realize all that's been lost and begin to make a plan to move yourself through the resultant fog. I tested negative for COVID seven days after testing positive, but two weeks later I was still sick. So, I did the obvious thing, I went to the doctor, but in retrospect I just had no real idea what I was dealing with or how devastating it would be. I was given steroids and antibiotics for an assumed infection, and I even committed to an extra twenty to thirty minutes of rest each afternoon. I doubled down on zinc and a bevy of vitamins, and I thought I was OK. I figured if I was patient, in a week or two, I would be back to grueling conference calls, doing joyful preschool drop-offs, and crushing it on my Peloton. I really believed this. Looking back, I should have known things were bad when I found myself suddenly sobbing, hysterically, in a BJ's parking lot after an optical exam, and couldn't tell you why. Turns out it was just one of the many neurological impacts of long COVID.

At its core, Gray Grief is a sustained period of pain—whether mental, physical, or both—and uncertainty about how to find your way out of it. I can't promise that it won't go on for way too long. I can't promise that it will ever end. So, you must find a way to live with it today. You begin to live with it when you recognize it and commit to owning it. You own it by acknowledging whatever the thing is that has upended your life and deciding to deal with it. You don't apologize for it, you don't ignore it, you commit to accepting it and finding a way to manage whatever the crisis may be. You need to recognize the most annoying and frustrating part about it, that things are different now.

It was April 29, 2024, when I entered my own season of Gray Grief.

Fuck. Well, this must be rock bottom.

As the lines turned darker and darker pink on my COVID-19 test, I raced around my bedroom, looking for a mask and reviewing the medications, tissues, and other provisions already contained upstairs. Matt was out picking up Bennett from school. I rapid-fire texted him, "I have COVID. I need a few minutes to get organized so please take him for lunch." It was 2024, and somehow I had COVID for the very first time. I had spent the last few years living life. Going on a book tour, visiting friends, eating out, attending concerts, traveling, and so on, and somehow had managed to avoid the damn thing until now.

For me, those pesky pink lines were so stressful and problematic not because I was worried about dying, or even long-term side effects of the virus, but because I was already sick. Earlier that year in January, I received the COVID vaccine booster. I got very ill for a few days—body aches, headache, congestion, and an exhaustion that felt like a combination of bleary-eyed early days of parenthood, food poisoning, and the flu. Then, less than forty-eight hours after I got the shot, I started having a period. For me it was a sign of big trouble. I have an underlying endocrine issue that means I've essentially been in menopause since my twenties so this sudden bleeding at forty-one made no sense. I bled on and off for weeks. I had a headache that felt like I was drowning. The booster had triggered a hormonal issue, which meant I had been in physical pain for months before getting COVID and was just starting to identify a solution to my health challenges when I got actual COVID. I felt like trash. I had no control over my body. I could barely even open my eyes. Seven to ten days later I assumed I would be fine. I figured, *OK. I must have hit rock bottom. I will begin my climb out of the abyss in a few weeks, max.* I really thought everything would be back to normal in no time.

The thing about rock bottom, it isn't a question. It isn't a "I guess this is it." You know when you are there because things have spun fully out of your control. You are in a space you can't simply escape; you instead have to *work* your way out. You are face down in the dirt, there are no neat and tidy solutions, there is just a long, hard slog toward something better. Whether it is being forced to declare bankruptcy or enter recovery, when you are there, you know you are there and something needs to change. It is the end of one state of being and the beginning of something new. You can't begin anew until you're face down in the aforementioned dirt, able to see what you're really dealing with: addiction, marital challenges, infertility, et cetera, and ready to construct a plan and fight your way back to where you belong. You can't do that until you own whatever it is you've been forced to deal with.

When the ability to control is lost and uncertainty arises, we have to find a way through its ever-shifting landscape. We must buckle up. If you're like me, you won't relinquish all control and go with the flow. Seasons of Gray Grief often necessitate a fair amount of planning, project management, and straight up work, so going all Zen overnight isn't going to cut it. If you're caretaking—it can require organizing schedules, assisted-living tasks, managing hospice nurses, medical treatments, arranging transportation for doctors' appointments, and so on. If you're going through a loss, it can require talking to lawyers, managing annoying family members, or planning a memorial service. You don't need to be some free-spirited, go-with-the-flow hippie martyr and it probably wouldn't help your circumstances. Whomever puts that pressure on you or if you're doing that to yourself, there needs to be a reality check. Playing it fast and loose won't cut it if you're inherently controlling or forced to be in charge of the circumstances. What we must do is navigate our own unique path through the dark.

I had a therapist right after my mother died who was fond of saying, "control the stressors you can control." At the time I was worried about my sister, who was living with bipolar disorder, and I was worried about my father, who I felt was drinking too much (ironic because I was too!). I arrived at her office on the Upper East Side and simply collapsed into the nice eggshell leather chair with a footstool. I droned on and on about things I couldn't fix. "He needs more help, but he's not getting it. My mom was always the most worried for him and now I see why. Is there anything we can do for Heather that will be enough now that mom is gone? And if she has another episode, what will that do to my dad right now? To her? How will I help her, living so far away?"

"Control the stressors you can control and let go of the rest," she said.

At the time it was annoying, but she was right. What I could do is tell my father about my concerns for him, and I did, and he responded with compassion and adjusted his habits. I couldn't change the fact that my sister had bipolar disorder and my mother's death was a destabilizing event, but I could figure out how to support her if she needed it. I could not wave a magic wand and suddenly have the grief and loss erased, but I committed to therapy, exercise, and journaling. In life there is always more that we cannot control than that which we can, even during "normal" times. We must preserve our time and energy for the things we can control when life gets hard.

We live in a grief-averse society that rarely discusses the pain and discomfort of grief and loss, so we definitely don't discuss nontraditional forms of grief. The grief that arises when your life becomes an uncertain and unpredictable terrain riddled with painful landmines that you have to navigate. The grief that arises in the midst of a divorce, chronic illness, job loss, violence, or political strife. The grief that arrives when everything in life is cloudy and unclear: Gray Grief.

Gray Grief by nature is burdensome. It is murky and suffocating. It is different from traditional bereavement when you lose someone you love, in the sense that, in traditional grief, there is a clear end to someone's life. Once they are dead, they are gone from this world. They can live on within you; you can continue to love them and feel their love in return, but they are not here and that is the end of part one of the story, and in part two you learn to live with their loss. Fin. With Gray Grief, there is a situation that upends your life for an extended period of time, possibly indefinitely, with no clear path forward and no known end date. It is akin to, but different from, anticipatory grief, when you know someone is going to die and you are forced to face that reality.

Gray Grief is grief that shows up when we have to alter how we live. It causes a fundamental shift in your identity that you did not choose. As I've mentioned, our identity is always in flux and it should be. We get in and out of relationships. We change careers. We relocate to new places. Those changes, in most cases, are our choices. They were an opportunity to exercise our personal agency, but it is Gray Grief when it is forced upon you. When your husband walks out and never returns. When you get laid off from the job you've held for thirty years. When mom becomes ill and needs your care for an indeterminate period of time. Or when a virus wreaks havoc and breeds uncertainty in your body.

Gray Grief is the pain you feel when you're forced to reckon with the space between who you feel you are meant to be in the world and your actual ability to participate actively in the world. Gray Grief is me wanting to light the world on fire with my words, but today being far too sick to even open my laptop. Gray Grief is me wanting to be the best mom ever, but today I cannot play cars or drive my son to the pool or pick him up because I am simply too weak. Gray Grief arrives every time I have to cancel fun plans with friends because I do not feel well. It's when I'm forced to acknowledge this painful thing, that is very much outside of my control. Gray Grief is the chasm between my pain and my potential.

In struggle, we must identify nontraditional, well-paced ways to measure progress. When the Green Bay Packers are down, my husband generally wants them to run the ball and carefully gain a few yards at a time until they score a touchdown. "Peck at the eyes" is the saying and the metric is a handful of yards at a time, no Hail Marys or anything fancy that can lead to penalties or turnovers, or in my case more time spent in bed because I overdid it.

Progress is measured by forward momentum but without a specific intermediate target. The goal is always to win the game, but that doesn't mean throwing the ball all the way down the field at every opportunity. It is simply a commitment to "move the ball down the field." That's what I want you to do.

When things are uncertain and progress is small, it can often feel like you aren't making any progress at all, but you are. Perhaps you haven't been on a real date since your breakup, but you're now open to the thought. When in the fog, figure out how to measure it in a realistic manner that doesn't make you feel bad about yourself.

At the advice of my friend Anna who also has long COVID but is thankfully almost fully healed, I wrote down everything that was hard for me—talking for more than thirty minutes, walking up our driveway, etc.—and then after thirty days had passed, I would assess them. For instance, on Halloween we went to our neighbors' for pizza before trick-or-treating and socializing, but I found that it was too much on my body. I left after an hour. By New Year's Eve, I could hang out for two and a half hours and by my birthday weeks later, it just wasn't as hard on me. I certainly was not well and nowhere near "normal Marisa," but I could socialize just fine for a casual birthday dinner at home, and I wasn't totally destroyed the next day. My progress was minimal relative to what I was accustomed to, so I had to adjust the metric to even see the progress.

I taught myself to identify my metrics and not what others expected of me: the ease with which I could walk around my house, whether or not I could make it to the mailbox without shortness of breath, and how long it would take me to recover following a visit with a friend.

Having clear metrics or milestones allows us to see the progress while in the dense fog of Gray Grief. I was moving forward; I just had to figure out what navigating it would look like for me.

Our brains want to feel like there is some stability, something solid to count on in our lives even if it is tiny. Metrics keep us from falling prey to despair. They reduce feelings of anxiety and helplessness. Gray Grief is something we will all have to walk through; the metrics allow us to get clear on what you can control when you're in it.

3

...Pain

Chronic pain is incessant. Like the TV is on in the background and you cannot turn it off. I'm not just talking about the pain in your body, when your joints or lungs don't allow you to move past illness but also deep and overwhelming emotional pain. Shame, failure, extreme disappointment, or severe anxiety. It is jarring, like when you're relaxing on the couch and your loved one is scrolling Instagram at full volume. It is unceasing. The pain is at a level of intensity that makes even breathing difficult. Mindfulness and maintaining a commitment to the present moment are impossible because the present moment is terrible. Every deep breath is a reminder of the pain that haunts you. Focusing on the present only draws more attention to the brokenness.

As a child, my father had a workbench in our basement, and 99 percent of the time it was a cluttered mess only he could navigate. Pretty sure this is still the case. One of the things I loved on that workbench was his vise. Operating the vise when he needed to use it was a fun privilege for a kid, but my dad would always have to follow behind me and tighten it more. I wasn't strong enough to apply the level of torque required to fully stabilize a piece of wood or whatever else he'd placed in there. My father would use his enormous hands to twist the lever on the vise well beyond my strength. This is what my head felt like the night I woke up from hours of drug-induced sleep, and realized a piece was missing from my night guard. In my sleep, I bit right through the damn thing. That's the thing about pain, there is often no real break from it, not even when you are unconscious and asleep.

One of the most difficult things to navigate about pain is that it puts space between you and everyone else. No one can fully understand your experience with pain whether physical or emotional. Our responses to pain are different because we are all different. We all have different pain tolerances and needs and reactions, and no one else can tell us how to cope with our pain. When I am in a great deal of pain, my husband comes to check on me, and I don't even know what to say to him. I consider, "I am in tremendous pain, and right now there isn't a thing you can do to fix it," or perhaps, "I don't know what to do with myself and I'm too sick to even cry," or when I'm really spiraling, "Am I a terrible person? Is that why it feels as if my head might explode? I know I can sometimes be a brat, but this is horrendous." We are both fixers, helpers, doers, and it pains him greatly to not be able to fix my pain, and for me not to be able to articulate to him how he can help. To be a fixer, a problem solver, and find yourself faced with a problem that you simply cannot solve can be disorienting. It's an assault on our identity. It freezes us and there is literally no release, or at best, very little. As he stands in the bedroom doorway or sits on the edge of our bed, I find myself reminded of the book by Khalil Gibran, *The Prophet*; there is a section on marriage I have always been fond of:

> *But let there be spaces in your togetherness,*
> *And let the winds of the heavens dance*
>   *between you.*

Perhaps this is a time when, like it or not, we are meant to have space between us. Perhaps I am meant to abide inside my own personal prison of pain and misery, separate not only from Matt, but from everyone I love. In this life no two experiences are meant to be the same. We are all on different paths and sometimes, you have to move forward or through things mostly on your own.

I don't blame Matt or any of my loved ones for their inability to understand my pain. The lights are out and this place is unfamiliar to us both. Eventually I hope to find light, and until then we are resigned to wait out the darkness till morning, because morning always comes. I don't know when my morning will come, so for now, I live in the dark.

Pain distorts your vision. Your vision of yourself, your vision for the future and what is possible for you, and what you deserve. Pain changes us. When pain arrives, I am not myself, forget my best self. I am unrecognizable to everyone when it begins to feel as though my head is stuck in that vise. I am no longer present in this world. No matter the time of day, I descend into the blackest and darkest of places. I think of it as the deep black-blue of the ocean depths that we would all be wise to fear. There is no end, there is no way out, there is no light; I am immersed in a vast, all-consuming and terrible place. The landscape is one I do not recognize. I am drowning.

I cannot communicate effectively, I am incapable of being a normal friend, I am adrift in a body that is no longer under my control, and all of those things are sources of grief. It changes my personality. The ever patient, understanding, flexible, and joyful wife, mother, and friend is replaced mostly by silence. My frayed nerves and pounding head cause me to lose my patience more swiftly at my husband and child. I am quick to judge and often angry. I don't know what to do, so I reach for distractions—edibles, retail therapy, social media; vices I know well enough in my forties to consume in moderation, but I'm not perfect, so I consume them. Anything to give myself a break from this period of incarceration caused by pain.

Pain also often brings with it unexpected feelings of doubt. I expected pain to cause frustration, anger, sadness and despair, but not doubt. I doubt my ability to get things done. I doubt my memory of things. I doubt my perspective. Is it really that bad? Have you actually done all you can to get better? Fundamentally, I doubt myself because I know I am not me.

Doubt is a fundamental part of being human. We are hardwired to ask questions and seek answers, especially when presented with new information. Before getting married, I doubted my ability to be "successful" or "good" at marriage. I grew up in the generation that heard over and over again that 50 percent of marriages end in divorce, and with statistics like that, why bother? I doubted whether or not I would do a good job as an adoptive mother. Is my heart large enough to hold a child I had no hand in creating or carrying? Of course it was, but it was also a period of challenge and uncertainty, and I wanted to ask myself the hardest of questions before committing to this human being forever and ever.

A healthy amount of doubt makes us smarter and more discerning and allows us to make better decisions. Doubt pushes us to analyze our values, motivations, needs and desires, who we are, and how we love, but self-doubt is different. Like some form of personal failing. I cannot fix this situation, which on its own is upsetting enough and now it is also causing me to doubt myself and my abilities, which is perpetually devastating.

The physical pain and ensuing mental anguish make me feel weak, and that's because I am. The doubt that arrived with the pain, pointed me to the truth. My body is not well. I doubt myself, because I should. I cannot trust myself in the same ways. I cannot be relied upon by others in the ways they have become accustomed to relying upon me. I cannot experience joy in the same way because pain is always present. I cannot even drive in the same way. The year I got sick, I was in a car accident. I was driving on the highway, returning from an acupuncture appointment. A state trooper cut off a vehicle a few hundred feet in front of me, which led to a very sudden slowdown and the Subaru two cars in front of me auto stopped. The car in front of me then slammed into the Subaru, and I rear-ended him. It was Easter weekend, and my brand-new car was nine days old. I haven't driven that far (about thirty minutes) since then because I doubt my ability to do so safely.

At the time, I knew I wasn't right. I knew I was in a lot of pain, but I didn't give myself an opportunity to take a step back and assess my doubt. Where was it coming from? Was it rooted in fact? Was it valid? What was it trying to tell me? My doubt was attempting to direct me to the seriousness of the situation. I was more than "in pain" or battling a headache that wouldn't go away. I was truly sick and needed to learn to live differently. I didn't fully understand the implications at the time, but I needed to do more than make doctors' appointments and do research to figure out what was wrong with me and how to fix it. I needed to question everything about how I lived, worked, and related to the world around me in order to begin to heal.

Pain does indeed have a purpose, but suffering does not.

While *hate* is considered a bad word in my house, I actually kind of hate people who try to force others to find meaning within their pain. They are grifters trying to sell you the equivalent of literary snake oil via books, conferences, and programs that promise instant cures or ways of reimagining your personal challenges. They want you to turn your lemons into lemonade, business success, or social media influencing. They also often make you feel like the issue is your fault so that if their "solutions" don't work, you can't blame them. It must be you that is missing some element of their recipe, and you better make that lemonade, or fail.

Our deep urge to make things better by making them more meaningful is understandable. It is rooted in a modern-day commitment to toxic positivity, keeping everything at a hundred, and strict emotional self-reliance. We are all expected to fix, or at least hide, our problems whether they be physical or emotional. We don't talk about grief, we don't ask for help, and we don't encourage people to simply accept the terror that eventually comes for all of us if we live long enough. Instead, we stick with this message: "I did it, so you can do it too," often coupled with a mentality that sends us down an *Alice in Wonderland* rabbit hole to create beauty from our trauma.

It disgusts me because it makes light of the fact that so many people did not choose their circumstances. They are in a state of perpetual suffering because of our lack of social safety nets and differing perspectives on who does and does not deserve to live a dignified life. When we refuse to show all people they are worthy by ensuring everyone has health insurance, quality pre- and postnatal care, access to reproductive care of all kinds including abortion, mental health support, and a living wage we create uncertainty where it does not need to exist.

When you don't know if you can afford your insulin, gas, and eggs in any given week, you are navigating uncertainty and suffering. In forcing you to turn your pain into purpose or a new business, or whatever, under those circumstances seems to deny or make little of your daily struggles. It is inappropriate, cruel, and harmful. I do not think anyone should be pushed or, worse, forced to make meaning out of their pain, or out of any form of loss.

I promise you there is a better way, and it starts with the truth.

The purpose of pain is to direct us to a problem. To some form of harm, hardship, or concern, whether it is spiritual, physical, psychological, or emotional. Pain shows us what is and is not possible for us. It alerts us to danger. It points to a deep and destabilizing loss of some kind. Whether physical or emotional, pain often arrives to limit us, to intentionally hold us back from living normally in order to create space for healing.

A few years ago, I supported my childhood friend Subrina through the decision to cut off contact with her mother. She was in pain for a long time. I watched her struggle for decades to try and build a positive relationship with this woman, but it only ever led to further harm. The pain she felt pointed her to the fact that, unfortunately, she was never going to get the love and care she needed or deserved from this relationship. She listened to that pain and walked away.

Oftentimes, the hardest to admit is that we must stay present with our pain in order to identify what we need from it. It is hard because pain makes the present moment miserable. All you want to do is escape. Instead, we need to sit still just long enough to get clear on what is happening inside of us. Your body, your spirit, your mind. When we stay present with our pain, we create space for that pain to show us what we really need and how to heal. You need to sit with it so you are able to clearly communicate with actual experts what is showing up for you, what it feels like, and where it hurts so you can help them help you. You need to sit still to contemplate various solutions and discern what might be best for what's next.

Many of us are instant problem-solvers. If life pops an issue into our orbit, within thirty seconds we're on top of the solution. We move quickly, and we're constantly thinking about what's practical and next. You must move back in with your parents to care for them even though they are driving you crazy. You don't deserve peace. You can't afford peace. They raised you, and now it's your turn to have it hard. This is the mindset of so many of us.

There were about a million things I could do for my headaches and different types of headache phenotypes, or presentations. I had lists and endless research focused on headaches. I was on the phone from 9:00 to 5:00 p.m., in between naps my body forced me to take, with doctors and doing research.

I found the greatest help when I started to sit still, often crying on the front porch, so I could accurately think about what was happening to me and identify the right neurologist and potential solutions.

My gut instinct at the time was that my current neurologist was not the right fit for what my issue was. I knew I had a "new daily persistent headache" resulting from post-acute COVID syndrome. In plain English, I had headaches at a level of seven out of ten or greater every single day following my COVID infection months prior. I had previously heard that Botox was good for migraines, so I started researching its application for NDP headaches as well and found a few studies showing the efficacy. One day, from my front porch while my son napped, I located a new doctor and was able to see her within a week, which never happens with neurologists; they are usually booked out for weeks or months. I liked her energy, and she immediately provided me with thoughtful and compassionate care. It took some time, but she agreed with me, and I got my Botox and my headaches started to improve.

Whatever you choose to do, please find time to sit and listen to your pain. Don't ignore your pain. That heartache from loss—people will say that there are seven stages of grief and that's just another way to say "Get over it." That won't make it go away, but it will always make it worse. That's why it's important to get to know the pain. Ask it questions, get to know its triggers and moments of relief. When it's not as hard or when it's so difficult to manage it feels like you can't breathe. If you're that caretaker sacrificing your entire life for another, when does it feel hardest? You have to spend some time with the truth. It speaks the loudest when you are quiet and not talking, distracting your way out of it.

Whether we like it or not, pain is an ordinary part of life. Yet we still try to run when pain arrives and that often causes suffering.

Pain is a broken leg; suffering is walking around on that broken leg. Pain that we attempt to ignore turns into suffering. Instead of listening and being attentive to our pain, we try to will it away. I would love to find a way to do this successfully, but it is impossible. Pain is anxiety, suffering is choosing to not go to therapy to alleviate it. Pain is losing someone you love; suffering is choosing to do nothing about the ensuing grief you experience. Pain is inevitable, suffering is often a choice. Suffering looks like frustration and anger because no one is helping you and you're doing it all yourself. Suffering says, "No one cares." Suffering isolates. Instead of asking for help, suffering is taking on all the burden alone. It is emotionally burying all other possibilities because you know best. You are the mother, daughter, caretaker, and shepherd of the issue and must bear it all. That is suffering, and we must run from it if we are to live better.

And as much as I hate the bastard, pain is indeed a teacher and a motivator, and many do find meaning in it. Whether pain is emotional or physical, it is often a transformative experience. If not for my mother's illness and death at such a young age and the ensuing grief, I might not be as clear and intentional in my values and priorities. I might not be as successful, or more importantly, as content as I've found myself to be in this life. How I live today is greatly influenced by the pain I experienced as a child and young adult. I won't say that I am thankful for it, because truly I would give up all the lessons to prevent my mother's illnesses and early death, but it would be disingenuous to refuse to acknowledge it.

The teachings of a broken heart, a deep disappointment, or a sick body are forever. They leave an indelible imprint on our psyche. Through the darkness and disorientation of pain, we are altered. Pain forces patience upon us because healing of any kind takes time. Pain teaches us to be more compassionate to ourselves and one another because compassion is a necessary component of living with pain. Pain teaches us how to live within limits, ideally without shame or embarrassment. The lessons pain provides are like a sprinkling of stars in the night sky. Not enough to see clearly in the dark, but just enough to remind you light does indeed exist.

If you are living with pain, you can assume that you are going to make mistakes, you are going to have a bad day, or days, so you must learn to treat yourself with kindness and gentleness, the core of compassion.

Pain forces discernment and prioritization. When your physical or emotional resources are diminished you have no choice but to get really clear with the truth about how you will spend your time and energy. This is not about meaning making, this is about being honest about the fact that there is power in pain, that the pain and suffering we experience in this life do have some utility. Our hurt, as much as it may suck, is not worthless.

If you are in pain, it is OK to simply be. Sit with your pain so you can figure out what to do about it. Accept that pain is a very normal part of life, and more often than not there is something we can do about it. Your broken heart may not heal; a loss may keep you sad for a long time. Healing and solutions often take time, but we can reduce our suffering by being honest about our pain.

4

Marathon...

"AHHHHHHHHHHHHHHHHHHHHHHH-HHH!" he screams at the top of his lungs as he runs full force into me for a hug. "Can you feel that love?" he asks, as he squeezes me tight, almost too tight.

"Oh yes!" I responded. "It is the *best* love and my heart is so full."

Welcome to the soon-to-be-trademarked Run and Hug, one of the first adaptations I allowed myself to create in the midst of my illness. Bennett stands at one end of our living room, I sit on the floor at the other end, and he runs as hard as he can, as fast as he can, into my arms. I have to be careful his head doesn't hit me in the chest as breathing is still hard, but I live for these hugs. They are lifegiving, they sustain me during a season of darkness. The Run and Hug™ was developed in response to the fact that I was unable to lift my toddler. He was three, so he didn't understand my physical limitations, but he knew that "Mommy is sick and will get better" and for now, we modify our routine. If he wants to be picked up, I have to meet him at his level and he has to meet me at mine, so we spend a lot of time together on the floor.

There were a lot of tears involved in this "invention." I am not just a mom, but "caretaker" is deeply entwined into my identity. I care for my family, friends, extended family, for folks in Bennett's school community. I care a lot, and I like to take care of people. As a result of having a sick mom as a child, I am an excellent caretaker, and I know it. I also waited for this kid for five years and he is the literal perfect child for me. Yes, he is also a pain in the butt toddler like all the rest. He doesn't listen. He sneaks out of his bedroom to watch TV under the guise of "checking on his parents." And he has a language issue. Not in the developmental sense. In that sense he is ahead of the curve and his language issue is in the sassy category. Just last night he called his father an asshole for playing with one of his toys, so trust and believe there is no such thing as a perfect child, but he is absolutely the perfect child for us.

Not being able to hold him. Not being able to pick him up and provide the comfort he is accustomed to when he gets hurt. Not being able to carry him when we are in a hurry or lift him up to put him into his car seat. All of these things hurt, greatly. Initially, they made me feel inadequate as a mother, but then I remembered my own mother. Her being in a wheelchair and homebound for a decent chunk of my life didn't make her a bad mom. It somehow made her even better for still taking care of me; no matter how sick she was, I never felt like I had less of a mother. Absolutely not. My mother was perfect and could parent better from a wheelchair than most parents can on two good legs.

In owning my condition, I had to face a very important fact about this life. Not everything can be fixed, some things simply have to be endured. If we want to endure well during uncertainty of any kind, we must find our way to acceptance, to our own form of emotional endurance which often includes some manner of adaptation. We find a way to make our life work under whatever circumstances arise, no matter how devastating. This is something I am relearning. Acceptance has to come first, and it can be hard to attain. We often don't want to accept our reality when bad things happen, or uncertainty arises. I don't want to be sick. I don't want to be in pain. I don't want to have long COVID, but this is my reality. I can do things to make it easier and more tolerable, but I cannot take it away.

When I was twenty-two, my mom was diagnosed with breast cancer, and I knew she was going to die and all I could do was endure her death. We had endured her illness most of my life. I couldn't change that she was now going to die. My amazing mother with multiple sclerosis now also had stage 4 breast cancer and it was devastating. To lose her after witnessing her pain was unimaginable. I was young and angry. I couldn't imagine anything worse in the world than having my mother taken from me. But when I'd sit with her in the present and realize the truth of how little time we had together, I had to adapt and improve our circumstances. I could help care for her to make this process a little more comfortable (and I did, proudly). I could take good care of myself (I did not). I could create room for joy in our household (of course I did!), but I could not change the essential fact that she would soon die.

Denial is honestly the best, until it stops working. I couldn't deny the truth that was happening to her. I am living a less extreme version of this today. When I envisioned my life as a mother, I knew I would spend plenty of time on the floor playing with a child, but I did not think I would be on the floor because of necessity. Because I was, in fact, too weak to stand. My legs felt like Jell-O some days. My arms, my Michelle Obama–wannabe arms, arms that have lifted weights since middle school, were simply too weak to hold my son. When I found myself in this space of illness, initially I chose resistance and denial.

At the outset, owning my sickness was just too much for me. It was upsetting, and it felt like too much uncertainty about my life and health to handle at once. I could not bear the questions that raced through my mind. If I was sick long-term, what would happen to my marriage, my family life, my business? There would be no way to support my family if I could not work, and what would happen to the place my son called home? I could not face those questions, so I did my best to power through until that became untenable. My lungs started to become so tight, not only was I wheezing, but oxygen wasn't circulating properly at all. It was a wake-up call, I had to adapt, or I was risking making myself worse.

If I am honest, I did not want to have a physical disability. My resistance was rooted in deep-seated ableism. Anything that weakened me or made me vulnerable didn't match the identity I had built. Owning my physical limitations made me feel less safe in the world. I liked at least being able to believe as a Black woman in a society that already makes you feel weak and vulnerable that I could care for myself. In my mind strength = safety. I was raised to be strong in every way, I have been trained to hit hard, and I can run fast if heaven forbid I ever need to. Suddenly all that physical strength and mental acuity was lost overnight, and I didn't know what to do with the weaknesses that remained. And unfortunately, instead of viewing disabled people as individuals we should look up to and admire in our society, we have made disability, or really anything outside of "normal" physical and mental abilities, bad. If you have one, there is "something wrong with you." It is rarely a matter of "we all arrive in the world differently and that is OK." Instead, we choose to treat and view disabled people in this country as less than. It is horrible, but you don't realize how horrible it really is until you become one.

We often view all sorts of nontraditional norms as brokenness. I have friends who have said the same about their divorce or single parenthood. That it's seen as something went wrong or is at fault and deserves to be pitied. I will accept empathy, but I did not ever want to be pitied.

It took a heart-to-heart with Rebecca, who is a friend, colleague, and disability justice advocate to realize at this moment, I was disabled. She asked me, "Does your illness change the way you eat, the way you dress, and the way you interact with your loved ones? If yes, then right now, you have a disability."

The answer was a resounding yes. I could only eat low-inflammation foods and had to eat on a strict schedule to manage all my medications and supplements. I had to wear compression clothing to support blood flow, and I didn't have a social life because at the time my lungs were too weak to sustain a conversation beyond thirty minutes.

I cried buckets during and after my call with Rebecca. My grief was tremendous, and it was made worse by an ableist perspective on life and the world.

I had to face the fact that disability, especially temporary disability, was not actually a "bad" thing. Deeply unfortunate? Sure. Unsettling? Definitely. Scary and overwhelming? Absolutely. But to call it bad means disability is bad and it simply isn't fair or moral or ethical to label an entire class of people "bad."

We hold very little space for disability as a society. We view disabled people as different, we "other" them, and we only do what is minimally acceptable to accommodate them, or we do nothing at all. Did you know houses of worship were excluded from the Americans with Disabilities Act? So, one of the places in this country that is supposed to be about welcoming and belonging actively excludes certain people from participating in activities. I felt this lack of accommodation most acutely as I navigated Chicago's O'Hare airport as a sick person. It was a devastatingly difficult experience, and it opened my eyes to all that I take for granted, even as a woman who was raised by someone who was disabled.

When it was my mother, I remember feeling shame and embarrassment when we'd go grocery shopping at Walmart and park in a handicapped spot. I didn't want to feel different, unless that difference was associated with excellence and success. I didn't want anything, even parking in a handicapped spot, to remind me that things were different. Our lives were altered by her illness. Instead of accepting and adapting, as my mother did, or at least as she appeared to, I fought back. I hung out in the land of denial and teenage angst, and I tried to find ways to exert control over my life. I stopped eating. If I am being honest, and I want to be brutally honest with you, I do not think, based on my understanding of others' struggles, I would call it an eating disorder as much as a very immature version of a hunger strike. Suddenly my family life had been plunged into uncertainty, and I did not like it. I just wanted things to return to normal. I tried to ignore it, and that did not work, and then I genuinely lost my appetite. As I saw the attention I received from my parents and felt empowered having something within my control, I kept going. I remember my parents outside of the bathroom door begging me to eat and to not make the leap and throw up my food. I realized in that moment how much I was scaring them and how much I needed to find a way, somehow, to be OK in our new life.

    I decided then and there that I couldn't make this situation go away, but I could do the work of making my mom proud of me. I could do well in school, go to a good college, get a good job, and actually help her.

I never fully faced my love of denial and hatred of weakness, but I was a child and I found a way to cope. As an adult, I've realized I like feeling different when someone is praising my accomplishments. I don't like it when I am equated as being less than, or not having the same value as another human being. In capitalism there is always a hierarchy, and I prefer to be near the top. I want all the money, all the praise, all the power and none of the weaknesses or challenges that come with a body that simply doesn't "work."

Illness, grief, pain, and disability have humbled me. At some point we will experience circumstances, issues, and struggles that cause us to question our worth in the world. When it happens, we have to find a way to adapt to our circumstances whatever they may be, and the first step is mental and emotional.

We have to shift ourselves out of a deficit framework. Doing so allows us to access our emotional endurance. I had worth even if I was unable to work some days. If I couldn't support a friend emotionally through a crisis with her spouse, or go to the grocery store, I still had worth. Worth does not come from utility alone, but from our shared humanity.

It is not a bad thing to desire utility, to want to be useful to others, or to have a purpose. Purpose and utility become bad when we attach too much value to them. When they are the only things that make us feel worthy. When you think the only way to help your children through hard times is by buying them stuff. Or to care for a sick loved one until you are emotionally and mentally depleted. That is not the only way.

We have to dig deep to find our value and identify a pathway to adapting to our circumstances and accessing a well of emotional endurance that exists within all of us. We are all capable of living through devastating situations. And when life is hard, the last thing we need is more work, so instead of figuring out how to live with whatever has come up for you, look for a guide. Examine your network of relationships and find someone else who has experienced something relatively similar and is either on the other side of the experience or is living well through the experience. Someone who can help you sort through whatever you're dealing with. Identify a "sherpa" and borrow their playbook. In my case, I had Rebecca, who I met when I was working in the White House. Rebecca spoke extensively about boundaries, advocating for yourself, and caring for your mind and body when it is different. She shared with me how she manages her health and her disability. She shared her pain. Knowing Rebecca, you would never know how much devastating physical pain she carries. Rebecca has achondroplasia, which means she is a little person. She has a level of self-possession without arrogance that I love.

On our call, she told me if I wanted to be OK, I needed to care for myself with intention and ferocity. I was unwell and if I wanted to heal, I needed to prioritize my care. No one was going to do it for me, and I needed to be ruthless when it came to my needs, and I needed to be kind to Marisa above all else. She could hear my frustration and said, "Let a bad day be a bad day and prepare for the bad days because more are always coming."

She told me to build a "disability toolkit." For the toolkit, she advised me to identify the things that can support me when bad days come. Fun snacks, a fancy heating pad, nice bath salts for a soak when my knees hurt, a good series to dive into on Netflix when my eyes hurt too much to even read, et cetera. She gave me permission to be sick and not try to be productive, as is my tendency, but instead just focus on being gentle and caring to my body.

Before my call with her, I was afraid of what I would lose by acknowledging just how physically weak and sick I was. If I told the truth, even just to myself, what might I be denied? What we all need to do when things get hard is identify our nonnegotiables and find a way to make them happen even in the midst of our limitations. For a long time, there was a lot I could not do: workout, work long days, travel, visit with friends, et cetera. I had to accept those limitations and losses. They hurt and I was moved to tears on many occasions and often felt left out, but there was one thing I refused to be left out of: motherhood.

Our son is adopted, so trust and believe that I worked too hard and too long for this child born from my heart and another woman's body, to have any part of motherhood taken from me. I had to learn to ask for a lot of help, but I was still going to mother this boy on my terms. There was no way I would be denied the right to hold him. We had to adapt because that was one thing I was simply unwilling to accept. After we created the Run and Hug™, I realized I was borrowing a page from my dear mother's playbook. Getting sick at thirty-seven with two young children meant she had to adapt early and often.

She was as type A as I am, so there were also a few nonnegotiables that had to be managed over the years. My mother was the ultimate girly-girl. She was vain just like me and loved clothes, hair, makeup, jewelry, all of it. One of her nonnegotiables was looking good. She cared about what she looked like till the bitter end. During the early days of her harshest chemo, her hair started to fall out. Before she lost it all, she called upon a friend to give her the cutest little curly-haired pixie cut. When her body became bloated by chemotherapy and steroids, she bought new clothes she could not afford. And at the end of her life, when she was too sick to leave the house, she had her hairdresser and a nail technician come over and do her hair and nails. I actually had to cancel one of her final appointments and let them know she was no longer with us. Beauty was her nonnegotiable till the end.

My mother taught me that when life changes, we must of course mourn what's been lost, but we then need to move forward and adapt. The common saying is "evolve or die," but in times of uncertainty it's "adapt or risk falling prey to despair." These adaptations allow you to hold on to key parts of your identity and the things that bring you joy. Identifying new ways of doing the things that matter most to us allows us to experience a comfort and joy during a chaos that is uniquely our own. The things that matter most to you are different from the things that matter most to me, but finding your way to hold on to them when life gets hard can truly be a lifeline.

On one of my sickest days, Bennett wasn't ready to get out of bed in the morning. When he's not ready, I have to be the one to get him. Daddy is too loud, enthusiastic, and impatient. This morning, as I sat on the edge of his bed rubbing his back, head throbbing in pain, I felt grateful. The simple act of mothering. Comforting a sleepy child is something I will always be capable of. As he climbed onto my lap and placed his perfect sweaty head onto my shoulder, I thought,

This I can do. No matter how sick I am, this is something I can do. I felt the deep well of love that I reserve for only him. I willed this child into existence, and he is mine.

We know there will be things like this in life—illness, death, hardship, suffering—but we can't really practice how to endure them until we are experiencing them. When I found myself day in and day out, waking up in pain. Each morning my chest so heavy it felt like it was filled with liquid cement, making it hard to move or breathe. My headache felt like a combination of the worst hangover of your life (the day after my wedding, in my case) and like it was stuck in that aforementioned vise, and no matter how many hours I slept each morning I still felt a bone-deep exhaustion that medically is classified as fatigue. Nonetheless, I would slowly climb out of bed, pull on my required compression leggings, sit down to brush my teeth (too weak to brush and stand up), then make my way downstairs to begin the morning rush of breakfast and getting ready for school. My husband would ply me with an espresso, but nothing was ever enough to beat back this exhaustion and as soon as my boys were out the door, I'd get right back into bed. I might not even have the strength to bathe till later in the day, I was so physically fragile. And yet, I had to keep running my business, writing this book, and caring for my family. It felt like I was suffocating. And when you feel like you are suffocating,

I want to remind you that endurance requires training, so go easy on yourself. As you adjust to your period of uncertainty you will have to adapt if you hope to endure. It feels like a never-ending marathon because it is, so treat it as such. Emotional endurance requires reimagining, creativity, and strength. I had to adapt and train if I was going to survive. I have this image of runners crossing the finish line in the New York City Marathon in my mind, something I will absolutely never do. No sane person got up and simply decided to run a marathon on that particular day in November. Everyone had to put in very serious training in order to be there. Long runs, short runs, collagen, extra sleep, carb loading, et cetera. It is basically a full-time job and the folks who actually win have been running daily, or almost daily, for years, sometimes decades. They can endure because they practice. No one can really teach us how to train for emotional endurance; it is something that has to be learned when you find yourself living with hardship and uncertainty.

5

...Connection

IN CLINICAL TERMS, loneliness is seen as the discrepancy between the preferred and the actual level of social interaction. It can have devastating consequences, as separation from social connections is often involuntary. In navigating our own personal periods of uncertainty and pain, it often feels as though we are separate from the world, set apart. It is so hard to be in the world, but not of the world. When navigating uncertainty—life when it's hard—it is a strange dance to exist in a life that is yours, but that you no longer recognize or connect with. Whether the lack of recognition, of connection, is long- or short-term, it deeply affects your spirit.

Some months into my illness, the loneliness became palpable. Connections, even with those I most deeply loved, often felt as though they were being stifled, or filtered through an impenetrable veil of pain. When stuck in the lonely orbit of struggle, your loved ones become children listening through a parents' door about your illness. They are concerned, confused, and worried. More often than not, they also just don't know how to help you.

Your loved ones know you're in pain, but even the closest people to you cannot put a stop to it. They must stand as witnesses to your period of personal challenge and hardship. And it's as hard for you to watch them watch you suffer. You are on an island all alone and that isolation can leave you at higher risk for depression.

You're forced to experience life and relationships through a filtered screen. Almost as if trying to decipher what someone is saying when you're underwater. There is an absence of ease in all your relationships. Your partner, child, family, closest friends, they can empathize, but they cannot fully connect with the experience you're having because they aren't living it. Sometimes you might have enough of being isolated from them. You recklessly try to break through— pretending to be OK enough to go to the birthday party or wedding while internally none of it feels joyful, but like pressure and anxiety and discomfort because your world is falling apart. You tell them it's OK that you've lost your job, reinforce that you will be all right. You know they "feel bad," but they also don't get it. There are some experiences—often the most difficult times—when they cannot reach you emotionally, nor you them. When your life feels so isolating and unnerving that it's hard to connect with those who care about you.

Our persistent inability to communicate the full extent of our emotional or physical pain to another human leads to a deep form of loneliness that we must learn to abide within.

These consequences can further worsen a circumstance that was already challenging. You're managing a divorce when you realize you feel lonely because you are the only person in your friend group who has ever gone through a divorce. It is a real shit sandwich to have to manage unexpected and challenging emotions during an already difficult time. While I have always enjoyed being alone, alone in my illness was different. It was not my choice to be alone, and this aloneness interfered with things I enjoyed like hosting dinners at our home or traveling to visit my girlfriends. It hurt because it was the connection I craved; I desperately needed female connection. All I wanted was to sit with my friend Adriana, who mind you worked very hard to stay connected from afar, but this was the longest we'd gone without seeing each other since we were eighteen. It was devastating. I just wanted to be with her, put my head in her lap, and let her mess with my hair. I just so missed the love and care of other women. My husband is wonderful and mostly flawless, but it just wasn't the same. I desperately missed my girlfriends.

And this wasn't just a physical longing; I was emotionally isolated from everyone because of what I was experiencing. This doesn't happen to me often, but one experience in particular does often make me feel somewhat emotionally lonely: racism. My close friend group is racially mixed, but mostly white and Matt is white too. As a Black woman with opinions on the internet, I have to deal with racist events that happen in the world and are covered in the news, and personal racist attacks simply as a result of being a Black woman who expresses herself in the world. My friends are deeply supportive, empathic, and racially aware, but they also know and will often admit that they don't completely get it. After George Floyd's murder, my husband said, "I will never fully understand your pain," and that was the most supportive thing he could have said. I know my people all love me and support me, but racism and racist violence remains an emotionally lonely experience for me.

With my illness, separateness was necessary. I needed hours of rest each day and the act of speaking caused shortness of breath. You may need to separate for other reasons that have nothing to do with physicality but space is required on your journey. Maybe you need space to process a deeply traumatic event alone before even sharing it with others. If you need space to heal or deal with something challenging, I want to encourage it. Loneliness is devastating, but stepping away from the daily pressures of life, relationships, and caretaking can be healing and much needed when hard times and uncertainty enter your life. Healing of any kind can sometimes require a fair amount of isolation. Whether what you are navigating is physical or emotional, you likely need a fair amount of space to recover from and process what you're dealing with.

    I still felt crummy about it. I would lie in bed watching *Emily in Paris* and stare out the window at our yard. The blue sky felt like a taunt as I navigated my personal period of darkness. As the seasons shifted from summer to fall and I was still in the same place, sick and in bed and moving on to a new show, *How to Die Alone*, a fear of missing out showed its face at the core of my loneliness. Loneliness was the pain; FOMO was the suffering. I've always enjoyed being by myself when it's been a choice. A good silent retreat, a solo meal, or a quiet stroll alone were all things I genuinely loved, but now that I was forced to be alone, almost all the time in pain, I desperately yearned for company. A fear of the rest of the world moving on without me became a very real feeling.

Every opening of social media left me feeling terrible about myself. I felt behind and off track and like I must be doing something wrong. I am lying in bed carefully calculating the number of steps I can take around my own house while a peer gives a TED Talk, and I can't help but feel like a loser. On social media, there wasn't much space for anyone to care that I was sick. Envy and resentment naturally developed and a simple scroll through social media could send me spiraling into a deep, dark hole of insecurity and inadequacy. I felt like if I didn't stay publicly in the world, sharing my work and actively contributing, I would be forgotten about. I was confident my illness would lead to fewer professional opportunities for me today and in the future. Full-on freak-out thanks to comparison and vanity. In the fog, it was easy for someone's life to look better than my current state. While I sat at home unable to even take a deep breath, they were on vacation hiking. While I felt and looked quite miserable, they had glass skin and looked better than ever. How did some people go most of their lives without tragedy or pain? They still had two parents who loved and supported them. People who get pregnant without even thinking about it. People who are never forced to navigate our healthcare system as a person in pain. I just didn't get it, and I tried to not think about it. I didn't want to feel jealous or begrudge another human of their good fortune. But at times resentment overflowed. It was embarrassing, and I'd put down my phone frustrated with myself for these thoughts, but I also couldn't transcend this experience like some sort of Black Buddha filled with peace and compassion for all.

It can be hard to not view our pain or misfortune as a failing or some kind of judgment that is being leveled against you. On days when it felt like my head might explode, I honestly just wanted to punch someone. Sadness, frustration, and a feeling of lack are real when you're in tough times. When the fog is so thick, you can't see straight because you're blinded by physical or emotional pain. You should not be expected to have the same normal feelings you had before this set in. If you had a train run through your house, it's hard to just sit there smiling. Your life has been turned upside down. You are allowed to feel angry, envious, and out of sorts. Anyone who tells you to go be quiet and pray or take a self-help course should honestly just shut up.

When our friends began getting pregnant and all of our own efforts just kept resulting in more disappointment, I was never not thrilled for my friends, but my feelings of envy were very real. There were times when I simply could not be around their children. I love their kids so much but sometimes I just couldn't bear it; it made me too sad. Two things can be true at once. You can be happy for others and sad for yourself and that's OK. Honestly, that's exactly what it means to be an emotionally mature human. To hold space for both side by side.

When people are able to do or have things that we desperately want but don't have, it hurts. That doesn't mean we aren't happy for others: whether it's their perfect marriage while yours is struggling, or perhaps it's their money and you haven't yet found your way financially. Whatever it is, you must find a way to hold both your frustration and pain and your joy for others authentically, simultaneously. It may require you to sometimes ignore another cheerful call from a friend who just purchased their new house, but you can do it, it's just not always fun.

I was reminded of what it was like when we finally did get our baby, because you know what? I still had the FOMO. It took so long to get to Bennett and there was a lot along that journey that prepared us emotionally to become parents, but I would not let us do anything to practically prepare for a child, especially near the end. I was so afraid of another massive disappointment.

The last thing I wanted was to navigate more grief. We'd already been disappointed for nearly five years without a baby. It was heartbreaking, over and over and over again. After each treatment, after every embryo that failed to develop, after each blood test showed my body still wasn't ready for a transfer, and ultimately after our pregnancy loss, we were led back to disappointment. It was redundant, but every experience ripped me open and started a fresh wound. Each disappointment more painful than the last. We knew adoptions often fell through, we knew our luck was not the best when it came to becoming parents, so the last thing I wanted was a fully furnished nursery equipped to welcome a baby we still didn't have. I had friends who did this and had to walk past that nursery for many months, so when Matt suggested we design a nursery, I was appalled. He had clearly lost his mind. Absolutely not.

We got the call about our son around 2:30 p.m. one brutally hot summer day, and I know this because I was in the middle of my weekly 2:00 p.m. therapy appointment when Matt interrupted me about the call. We had him in our arms the very next day by 4:00 p.m.

We had exactly three things for a baby I had purchased years prior from the White House gift shop when I worked for President Obama. A hoodie, a bib, and a stuffed Bo dog. We were in no way ready for a newborn, but thankfully our entire community, including the people who are publishing this book, stepped up to support us. I was terrified we had missed something along the way or would be more inclined to do something "wrong" simply because we hadn't had time to practically prepare for his arrival. When I expressed this fear to a friend, she told me I needed to stop and instead of focusing on the parts of our experience that were different in a less-than-ideal way, I should instead focus on the positive differences between our story and everyone else's, and that's exactly what I did.

The thing about **FOMO** is it leaves little space to acknowledge the difference, good or bad, in each of our experiences in this life. The fear is rooted in comparison, but you should really only compare things that are similar, like two different types of apples. Obviously no two lives are exactly the same. There is nothing to compare. All the things we struggle with—insecurity, envy, lack, and loss of control—are rooted in thinking we should do life like everyone else. Your parents were together for forty years, so you and your husband should be. Your friend's cancer healed, then your illness should too. Your cousin went back to work two weeks after losing their job, so you should be able to do the same.

This fear doesn't connect you to others—it separates you—and feelings of loneliness and isolation grow bigger. When we let **FOMO** rule, we remain locked in a state of comparison with others, and for what? Someone once said to me, "comparison is violence," and it is. Does everything in life really need to be a competition? A game where you stack yourself up against your so-called peers, or are we all meant to be on our own unique journey? When we stay locked in a state of FOMO rooted in the assumptions we have about someone else's life or success relative to our own, we cut ourselves off from that person. We remove the ability to deeply connect with them and instead only communicate through a veil of assumption. You cannot build meaningful relationships this way and when you are mired in uncertainty and life feels heavy and dark and you're drowning, you need those meaningful relationships.

These feelings of FOMO can also cause you to doubt yourself and your abilities. While ill, I felt a vast expanse between my potential to contribute to the world, my unyielding desire to participate in the world, and my inability to actually be in the world. I have built a life and career that I love rooted in helping others thrive during grief and uncertainty and making the world a more just and equitable place. To be stuck in bed, turning down speaking engagements, writing opportunities, and client work because I was too sick to do it, was devastating. I want to be in the world. I have worked hard to create a life full of intention and joy and most of it vanished overnight. Thankfully, I still had my family, and I was still able to provide, but none of it was the same and none of it was enjoyable. There was simply too much pain for there to be much joy. Most days I went from bed, to getting my son off to school, back to bed with maybe an hour or two of work, all conducted from my bed. Forget functioning,

I was barely surviving. I was held in this space of tension, like opposing ends of a magnet, where I simply could not move. I could see my potential and I was very clear on what I wanted from life, but I couldn't actually reach it. The tension was unyielding.

The tension came with a deep sense of urgency. For better or worse I am someone who feels a "life clock" loudly ticking in the background. I know our time here is limited and we will all always only wish for more. I know this because I've lived one half of it. I am the daughter of a woman who first got sick at thirty-seven and died ten days after her forty-ninth birthday. During my sickest year, I was forty-one. Ever since my mother died, I've held tightly to an intense commitment to living life fully. When a parent dies young, it unlocks something within you. You cannot help but wonder if it will happen to you. "What do I really want from this life?" This question and my commitment to living with intention have led to some of the best decisions I've made in this life. The world, God, whoever you want to blame had taken my person, the person who loved me the most in the world, and now I was going to get what was mine. I started with a job working for President Obama as a senior adviser at the Small Business Administration, which I parlayed into a role as a deputy director in the White House, where I launched an initiative that is now a part of his foundation. My grief suddenly launched a whole new career. A deep commitment to healing from the loss of my mother ultimately inspired my first best-selling book *Grief Is Love*. I needed to do something with my pain. The pain of that loss built my emotional endurance and provided a level of steadfastness that allowed Matt and I to work through years of infertility and loss until we got to our son. Loss is a great motivator, but it can also be a hindrance.

When feelings of FOMO arise, sometimes we push ourselves to do more. We tell ourselves, *Yes, things are a mess right now, but I can still deliver the speech and attend that conference, it won't be too much to take on.* Then we take it on and find ourselves even more overwhelmed and we sit at the event and think, *This isn't really where I belong*, but by then it's too late to do anything about it. Now you're even more exhausted and overwhelmed than before simply because you were trying to quell those feelings of FOMO, but that's just not how you do it. Hard times have allowed me to see that living a meaningful life is not about doing the *most*. And doing the most in the midst of uncertainty is how we destroy our power. Doing the most isn't about exercising agency, but about living in fear and living at war with your circumstances and surroundings. Navigating uncertainty works better when the approach is "slow and steady wins the race."

Oftentimes, we continue to do the most when we are already at capacity for one reason or another because we are afraid. We are afraid that if we don't keep on keeping on as we've always done, we will lose. We will lose money, business opportunities, relationships, et cetera. And all of that may be true. When I lost my mom, I definitely lost some of the people who I thought loved me and when I got sick, I even lost a client. But when we are in a season of uncertainty, we must sit quietly in an uncomfortable space and make really hard choices. Are we going to choose to prioritize ourselves and build a meaningful life that is truly meant for us, on our terms, or are we going to choose scarcity, and make our situation worse by acting based on fear, continuing to do "all the things" and letting our pain exist in a void.

Living with uncertainty has taught me that a meaningful life is about honoring our physical and emotional needs by being present with them and thoughtfully caring for ourselves when life gets hard. It is about being honest about not only our feelings, but about what specifically matters to *us*. We often feel off track in this life, because we are. We are off track first because we have confused the terms of the track itself and second, because we are often looking at someone else's track and confusing it for our own.

We let FOMO overwhelm us and we apply undue pressure to ourselves because we feel like we have to do everything: be the rock star soccer mom, all-star boss at work, and most amazing social media–worthy wife. And when uncertainty arises and you're underwater you cannot be any of those things and you feel bad about it. You feel like you are messing up and social media basically exists to prove you are messing up, but you're not. You are being human and doing the best you can navigating a difficult period. You may only have one life, and you probably won't be able to do everything you want to in that one lifetime, but you don't get just *one* shot at the things that really matter or the things that are truly meant for you. You can have more than one career. You can have more than one shot at romantic love, and marriage if it doesn't work out the first time around. In your relationships with the people you love in this life—your children, your friends, your parents, et cetera—you get more than one shot to get it right.

We tell our kids to try, try, and try again but as adults we often carry around this sense that if we make one mistake, one misstep, or have a year or two of personal or professional setback, all our chances at community, success, or joy are ruined and that is simply a fallacy. I can still take my son for bike rides, just not this year. I can and will expand my ability to do grief work, but not this year. I will reengage with my friends in a more active manner, but not this year. And none of those things are easy to accept, but it is OK; actually it is normal to not be in a position to do and have everything you want, exactly when you want it. When we have to manage a lot of *not now*s it is a part of growing up.

As I sat quietly with my feelings of loneliness and FOMO, I came to a heartbreaking realization, that some of my fear was also about being forgotten. I didn't want people to forget about me because I was no longer physically out in the world. No fancy dinners or parties, no networking events, no conferences, no playdates with friends' kids, nothing. I just couldn't do it and I genuinely worried that in not engaging, by literally not being able to do these things, I would fall by the wayside and be forgotten like a piece of trash on the side of the road, blowing aimlessly. That's what I thought would happen to me. The desire to belong and to live a life of meaning and purpose is innate. When we feel either our sense of belonging begin to slip or meaning begin to vanish from our lives, our brains go into free fall and we become riddled with anxiety and if we aren't careful, a very real depression starts to set in. These feelings are often magnified when we reach for the distraction of social media. It does not actually help us feel like we belong. More often than not, it just magnifies those feelings and dangerously validates them.

When I looked on Instagram and saw friends, acquaintances, and colleagues, doing things I would normally do, and going places where I would normally be, I forced myself to get honest about why I felt bad. Most days, I'd rather scan my backyard for animals, play with my son, lounge on the couch, or go out to dinner with my best friend than attend any of the events I was "missing out on" on social media. I didn't actually want to do a ton of that nonsense, but I still wanted to be invited. I wanted to be included. Like everyone else, I wanted to belong. I was so sick and scared and overwhelmed, and felt like I didn't belong anywhere, not even in my own body. The loneliness was like a dark cocoon I knew I would one day emerge from, but when?

As humans we are meant to be in community and when chaos and uncertainty descend it can be both hard to be with and around others even if that is what you desire. You may be too busy caring for your ailing father to maintain your friendships. Perhaps your divorce is all-consuming, or layoffs are looming at work, and you need to focus on keeping your job, not keeping up with your friends. But according to self-determination theory, all humans have three universal psychological needs associated with growth, fulfillment, and well-being. One of these needs includes the sense of belonging and feeling cared for and connected to others, or *relatedness*, which is the term researchers often use. It is human nature to miss out, we all fear not belonging and being forgotten. Real or perceived lack of belonging can be deeply harmful.

We all need to identify our own ways of managing this particular form of anxiety. I started setting limits on my social media apps. I have friends who regularly delete the apps all together for weeks or months at a time and invest their scrolling time into actually connecting with other humans.

Become clear on what matters to you, and you alone, and leave little room for comparison with others. Be very clear about your intentions and priorities. Those things may fall off track as well, they often do, but when you're feeling adrift, disconnected, or forgotten about during difficult times that you're navigating it's easier to find your center.

Loneliness, social isolation, and a fear of missing out are all a normal part of navigating a difficult personal experience. When it happens to you, make a commitment to owning your feelings and reestablishing a connection with those who love you and support you. Do not let fear feed your isolation.

6

Light...

When I got into Gerald's (my regular driver's) car that day, I was headed to Paris for five nights with my crew of lifelong friends. Not for work, or a family obligation, but for me and me alone. Paris is for me, what Disney World is for your child. It has always held a sense of magic, wonder, and awe. It has all my favorite things: fashion, sugar, cheese, beauty, and a side of culture if you're interested. Cafés where you dine alone and still feel like you're in the middle of things. Grocery stores that stock lipstick in the most perfect shades of red. Pain au chocolat for breakfast every day, and raucous nights that often end in the early morning hours. And of course, the shopping. The. Best. Shopping. So many wonderful things you either can't get in the States or that would cost at least twice as much if you tried. When you add in the history of Black American literary and cultural excellence that is connected to Paris, it is enough to make this girl swoon. I am a proud New York girl first and foremost, but Paris will always be my mistress. So, when one of my best friends, Adriana, asked if I might consider joining her for a fortieth birthday trip to Paris, I couldn't say yes fast enough.

Adriana is someone who can make anything more joyful. That girl has a relentlessly, almost annoyingly positive, enthusiastic attitude about virtually everything. She has an infectious spirit and is one of the leaders of our crew. We all signed on for this trip to Paris because we knew she would make it a memorable and life affirming experience for everyone, so why was I crying on the way to the airport?

Long before long COVID even entered my awareness, I found myself in a different season of uncertainty. As I rode away from our home, headed to the airport for my flight, a large part of me felt like I was a disappointment to my family, but a smaller, quieter piece of me was elated. Nonetheless I still felt like a selfish asshole. As I headed to Paris, my mother-in-law was in Green Bay, Wisconsin, dying from stage 4 breast cancer. The same thing that killed my own mother fifteen years prior.

Before her cancer diagnosis, I spent the majority of our relationship trying to get my mother-in-law to like me. She was never mean, or unkind, she just didn't seem to have an interest in me, which I honestly found baffling. This was a bullet to my ego—I have been told since childhood I am a deeply likable human, and apparently that really meant a lot to me. This is what I said to myself and my friends after every visit with her. I'm a skilled relationship manager—it is literally what people pay me to do professionally! "You attract more flies with honey than vinegar," my father would say and that was my religion. I could lead a congregation on kind, compassionate relationships, and have a well-tested ability to see everyone's side in a conflict. As an adult, I truly know how to establish real relationships with pretty much anyone anywhere, but with her, I only ever faced disinterest and rejection.

Year after year, we would return to Green Bay, my husband's hometown, and I would make plans to spend time with my mother-in-law, Marcia. I would encourage Matt to go golfing with friends, and I would prepare to take her out to lunch or to the legendary Green Bay farmers market, but always at the last minute, she would cancel on me, usually via my father-in-law. I did not take it personally, and eventually, I became very fond of a handful of coffee shops and restaurants in downtown Green Bay where I would hang out alone for hours. Initially, it felt like rejection. Why didn't she like me? What am

I doing wrong? What might allow us to grow closer? I could never crack the code, so I just decided to choose acceptance. I knew from my husband and his difficult childhood and strained relationship with her that this was not something I should take personally, so I let it go. I was not getting what I wanted but I would continue to love and support her for however long she was in our lives. This was absolutely not the relationship I wanted, but this was Matt's mom and I would love her even if I never felt her love in return. Due in part to the complexities of our relationship with her, the prior loss of my mom, and her devastating diagnosis, the months leading up to her death were some of the hardest in my life, in Matt's life, and in our marriage. He was forced to grapple with the complicated legacy his mother would soon leave behind, the love and lies that were a cornerstone of their relationship, her ongoing illness, and her pending death.

    I held the trauma of watching him go through the worst thing that had ever happened to me, and I carried a lot of anger and resentment. A boatload of rage, to be precise. We worked so hard to show up for this woman who we cared for, but who had never, not once, shown up for us. She was not the surrogate mother I'd hoped for. She did nothing to support us through years of infertility and loss. She wasn't there to help when we finally did bring our son home. I was angry that his mother was getting all of these moments and memories with our son that my mother never had. We were both heartbroken over how much pain she was in and deeply saddened that our son would grow up without any grandmothers. But regardless of our shared and independent anger, resentment, and sadness, we wanted to show up in a way that honored our personal values of kindness and compassion, and the love we held for her.

Our family life felt like a constant battle to simply stay afloat, as we were repeatedly pulled under by anticipatory grief. I felt trapped. I was suffocating under the weight of my life. We just never seemed to be able to gain ground and I needed a break. I felt he did as well, but he just didn't feel comfortable taking one. A combination of guilt, *Why should I have fun when she is suffering and dying?* and fear, *As soon as I get somewhere, she is going to die*, kept him at home, but I needed to go. I was drowning and I needed out.

If you are in an extended period of emotional overwhelm, I want to encourage you to carve out room for the things that feed you. And not every experience needs to be as over the top as a birthday girl's trip to Paris, but I need you to do something that makes you feel a little bit better.

When I had long COVID, one day I knew I needed a break from being the sick version of Marisa. I could not go to Paris or even far from home because

I was too weak. So, I made an enormous cocktail and walked over to the neighbor's for her birthday party. She is almost a decade younger than me, and it was a field day–themed bash replete with tug-of-war (my team lost), a karaoke machine, and a giant inflatable waterslide. When Mariah Carey's "Fantasy" blared out over those speakers, I destroyed that mic.

My friend Krishan's mom loved horror movies. Totally incongruous with her actual personality, but she loved them. If she were navigating a period of uncertainty, I would tell her to carve out time to watch a thriller she enjoys every few weeks as an ode to her mom. These moments can feel like an indulgence or insignificant, like something you need to be able to justify, but they are more than that. They are the fuel you need to keep going. Your brain needs breaks from the pain, and you need to find ways to feed and energize yourself to move forward healthy and whole through the darkness of uncertainty.

By May 2023, Adriana's birthday, my mother-in-law had been living with stage 4 breast cancer and a host of complications for over a year. I felt like I was constrained. Like I was stuck in this place of great tension and pain that I simply could not break through. I was walking around with a weight on my chest and cement in my shoes. Anytime I wasn't with Matt, I was convinced that was when she would die.

I would be in Bennett's room putting him to bed and hear Matt walking quickly through the hall and say to myself, *He's coming to tell me she died.* Sadly, thankfully, anticipatory grief does not last forever because that is no way to live.

As the support person for Matt and in my case, also as a grief "expert," there was so much pressure, some self-applied, to be the best possible caretaker. I wanted to give Matt even more support than I had when I lost my mom. I wanted to simultaneously be the best mom ever to Bennett so Matt would have less to worry about. I wanted to be there for him in every way possible, simply because I love him and in the midst of it all, it felt like there was little to no room for me. My feelings, my needs, my concerns, had to come second to his—and as a wife or life partner that is what makes sense. However, that didn't mean it wasn't hard.

I missed my partner who was in the middle of his mom dying and yearned for us not to be in this place. Sometimes my own grief needed me. I had no interest in dealing with complex emotions; most days I was desperate to run away from it all.

This roaring need to escape was not independent of my love for Matt and Bennett, but it was integral to that love. I could not continue to show up in a way that honored the love I have for Matt, if I didn't take a break from it all. Being in a home consumed with anticipatory grief, waking up in the morning to the sounds of him crying, knowing my son wouldn't have any grandmothers once we got the call… I *needed* to go to Paris. The Paris trip was my oxygen mask. Without it, I would break.

Yet, even as a grief expert, I still heard the annoying voice in the back of my head. The irritating, unnerving bitch that would ask, *Why are you the one who deserves a break when it's his mom who is dying? How could you possibly be so selfish? Can't you just suck it up?* I've been down this road before, dealt with this voice all my life. I am very good at self-criticism—aren't we all? I am sure you are familiar with this judgmental bitch pushing you to be stronger, to do more, especially if you happen to be a caretaker. When I was younger and wanted to travel, the voice said I should be at home to take care of my sick mom. Now when I'm buying my totally awesome Beyoncé temporary tattoos the bitch says, *How do you know you won't be too sick to go to the concert?* This voice is not our friend, so stop listening to it.

Due to this voice, many of us choose to suck it up. We skip the big trip with friends (I did this when my mom was dying); don't buy the ticket to the concert; text our best friend that we can't make it because mom may pass any day even though it's been a year versus a week away. At the end of the day that voice doesn't know more than you do. You may not be able to predict the future, but you do know what you need, so please take it.

I know grief, so I know I could not just "to-do list" my way through this. In the meantime, I promised myself I would take a break from grief. I needed joy.

The psychology term *allostatic load* points to the fact that cumulative stress worsens your health. I knew if I just kept going and going, I wasn't going to make it. I had made this mistake before. When my mother was dying I completely lost myself. I was consumed by grief and caretaking, and I have no regrets for how hard I worked to care for her, but doctors believe my infertility was caused by the stress, trauma, and exhaustion of that period. I would not be doing that again.

While we waited for Marcia to die, I couldn't sleep. We may not have been close, but I still worried about her pending death. I worried about her pain and suffering. I worried how it would impact Matt. I worried about my father-in-law. Even though we never had a real relationship, I still loved her. Perhaps by default, but that's still love, isn't it?

As she died, I was reminded that "in sickness and in health" isn't just about the health of your spouse, it's also about your capacity and theirs when one of you is navigating a crisis. When we first started dating, Matt supported me as I worked through my grief over the loss of my mom. Together we navigated three prior cancer diagnoses with our remaining parents, worked our way through infertility and pregnancy loss, and the adoption process. He has stood alongside me throughout moments of immeasurable grief. Now my grief had to take a back seat to his, but does that mean surrendering solely to suffering in this season? I couldn't fully escape all of this pain, so I instead asked myself, *What might it look like to grieve well?*

No matter how complex your feelings may be, no matter how triggered, no matter how resentful, every single one of your feelings are valid, but they are also your responsibility. Grief, anger, resentment, envy—we often feel like an aberration for even experiencing them, but why? We have language for these things, we know they are real emotions that loads of people experience, so name them, own them, and decide what to do about them so your wait for dawn is easier. In naming them, no matter how uncomfortable they may be, we reduce their burden over us.

So as we waited for his mother to die, I grieved the loss of my husband. He was here, but he was not present. I have never been so lonely in the context of our relationship. No one tells you when you get married that there are a million different ways to lose a partner both temporarily and permanently. I'd temporarily lost my partner to his grief, and I made the choice to be OK with that. Because, what else is there to do? That is what marriage is all about. It is so much more than love and joy. It is a sacred commitment to another human being that you maintain *especially* when life gets hard. And Matt was doing all the usual Matt stuff. He took care of our kid, did all the family laundry, and channeled his anxiety into new home projects—painting our bedroom, removing the painfully tacky chandeliers that adorned most of our home, and doing a bunch of other things that I don't know anything about, but that are required to maintain and care for a house. But he was often emotionally unavailable. He did not have capacity for me and my feelings, and that would need to simply be OK. And the same would be true for him a year later when I fell ill and my capacity for him and his feelings diminished. Marriage isn't about all things being equal all the time. In a "fair" and happy and fulfilling partnership the scales are almost always tipped toward one side. You just have to make sure they don't stay one-sided forever.

If you are partnered or managing extreme stress with another human, that can make it feel impossibly harder. Dyadic coping methods are used for effective stress communication, empathic responding, and active engagement around the stressor. Dyadic coping methods essentially involve active listening when your partner conveys stress, some form of empathic response, and support around how to manage the stressor. If your wife comes home and shares information about a stressful situation at work this would mean you listen, ask thoughtful questions, and help her manage the stressor in an empathic and supportive way. During periods of loss or stress, having these tools can help couples, siblings, or friends navigate stress together in a healthy and productive manner. Fundamentally, you have to find a way to recognize what you're both holding and communicate often about how to get through it together and what each one of you needs.

And it is not easy. By the time Adriana's birthday trip arrived, we'd been living in this unhappy mess for fourteen long months. Anticipatory grief often feels like Sisyphus rolling the boulder up the hillside. You make a bit of progress, have a good day, and then there's no growth on the latest PET scan, and as soon as you start to have hope that they might last longer or somehow be that one in a million case that remains stable or reverses course, the boulder rolls back down the hill and crushes you. I felt like I was holding our little family together with Scotch tape and it was so exhausting. I had to get out.

In stepping toward joy, toward light, I knew I was also fortifying our marriage because resentment has the power to spread and create cracks till the entire foundation of your relationship crumbles. I would not let that happen to us. *We would not let that happen to us.*

Paris could fill me with love and laughter and hope and the support of amazing friends to help me cope with what was to come. It would also just make me happy and while my grief may have had to take a back seat, and life at home may have been miserable, that didn't mean I had to be miserable. I needed my friends, and I needed to pause the relentless caretaking. Joy feeds our contentment and keeps us from slipping into despair.

You need to take a time-out, and press pause, let a little bit of light in and step into a place of happiness, even if for just a couple of hours, when life feels full of sucks. You may not be able to take the pain away, we usually cannot, but a momentary respite from the hellscape will go a long way for your health and soul.

And when navigating global uncertainty and instability, whether around politics, recessions, war, famine, or the climate crisis, you need to be mindful and actively manage those external stressors as well. Compounded on what we're experiencing as a collective society, there's what is happening in our homes and private lives. All of this matters and it all adds up. Your grief or pain isn't sitting in a vacuum, it's walking around with you at work, interacting with people in your day-to-day at the coffee shop or as you sit in traffic. When you take care of yourself, you are helping others. You are also modeling what is possible when life gets hard.

If it is a vacation you need, take it! Grief vacations are 100 percent a thing. If it is financial uncertainty that you are experiencing, find ways to feed yourself that aren't costly. Start a new workout regimen to manage your stress, take a free class at the JCC, or launch a meditation routine. If it is depression, in addition to therapy and medication, could you go be consumed by a cool exhibit in a museum, or binge a funny series for the day to help raise your spirits?

We cannot just go and go and go and assume that we will make it through a challenging period unscathed. The science is clear: When stress arises we need to manage ourselves differently and that includes making room for breaks. It is a step beyond self-care.

For me, this is an act of self-preservation. Your body and brain will be clear with you when they need a break. To navigate a period of darkness and uncertainty well, you have to feed your light. You know when you are breaking. I know myself, and I've seen enough grief and heartache to know when I simply cannot take anymore. We all do, and when we feel ourselves begin to break, we have to do whatever we need to do to be OK.

I had to go away and let others care for me and stop caring for others myself.

As I planned for the Paris trip, I committed to doing whatever I could to make Matt's life easier in my absence. I prepared meals, set up additional childcare, and I wrote him a letter in case Marcia died while I was gone. I wanted him to know at that moment how sorry I was, and how much he means to me. I gave his parents and my brother-in-law a heads-up so they'd know to call me if something did happen. I remained committed to my responsibilities to my family before, during, and after my trip. I checked flights back from Paris to New York City so I would know which airlines had the best options to get me back quickly. I prepared a document of next steps for when she did pass, given I was the person who was delegated responsible for her memorial service. I informed his best friend, Scott, who lost both his parents before twenty-five, someone who I knew I could trust to show up if something happened while I was gone. And then I started packing.

I ordered "necessary" last-minute wardrobe upgrades for nights out dancing and comfortable shoes for days spent walking the streets of Paris. I researched options for gluten-free pastries. I may be off gluten but no way was I missing out on a croissant in Paris! I filled a carry-on with books I wanted to read instead of snacks and toys for a toddler. I popped an edible and headed for the door after one final goodbye. "I love you."

"I know," he said. "I love you too. Have fun."

No matter how much we love others, if we don't love ourselves first and best, it just doesn't work.

If you are a support person in this season of a relationship—whether a spouse, child, sibling, or friend—please remember that you need to press pause. You need joy, levity, laughter, and light.

I knew I'd likely return to some degree of frustration, sadness, and resentment because it was his mom who was dying and that's a hard thing, but I didn't let that keep me from going.

I ran away to the City of Light. I was greeted by cheers and hugs and snacks when I made my way to our temporary home in the sixth arrondissement. Their joy was a reminder that I'd made the right decision. In Paris, to quote the feminist icon Audre Lorde, "the love of women healed me." I was made whole again by my friends, *my family*, who have been in my corner for twenty-five years. We transitioned from girls to women and in some cases, mothers, together. We have shown up for one another through the ordinary ups and downs of adulthood and the tragic moments as well. In Paris, I took photos with them in the *Amélie* booth in Montmartre; we climbed to the top of the Eiffel Tower; I fell asleep head to head with one of them at the ballet (I am not sorry, it was a bad ballet); and was enveloped in their cheers as we squealed at the topless ladies at the world famous Crazy Horse Cabaret. I sat alone in a café one morning and worked on this book while enjoying an espresso. It was peak Black girl in Paris, and I was even mistaken for a

Parisian! I lounged in Turkish spas, consumed terrifying amounts of cheese, danced along the Seine, but most importantly, my friends breathed life into me. The focus shifted from my home to their children and careers, relatives, marriages, triumphs, and challenges. I got to listen; there were no expectations of me to contribute. I relished in hope for someone else. It was glorious. The City of Light fed my light and I was filled with joy.

You deserve to be too.

7

... Love

As your priorities shift during a period of uncertainty, you also have to reassess and establish new boundaries. Boundaries have become a nebulous thing often divorced from research and data. The advice we receive around boundaries usually centers on saying no and putting yourself first. There is little room for nuance or honest conversations about the very real commitments and obligations that many of us hold for other human beings who we care deeply for and in some cases are also responsible for. Boundaries are about so much more than saying no. At their core, they are about love. You cannot survive uncertainty without a deep well of love and compassion first and foremost for yourself.

As someone who has been a caretaker from the age of thirteen, I've always struggled with boundaries. If someone needs my help or support, I want to do it, period. In my mind, someone who doesn't want to help others is selfish and a bad person. At least that is what I used to tell myself, until I became the person who needed to say no to someone they love in a time of great need.

The text message arrived during my son's nap time. Our boy, proof that hope, love, and hard work do sometimes work well together. For years I felt this weight on my chest where his head belonged. A knowing that existed in my bones long before we began our journey to parenthood, that told me I was meant to be a mom. This child isn't just mine; *he is me.* My heart wasn't just full, it finally felt whole. I was so happy as a mother and dove headfirst into the joy and terror that is mothering.

I am so thankful for him, but as I collapsed onto our bed, bone-deep exhausted and emotionally spent from toddler activity, an alert pinged on my phone, a text message that I didn't want to receive. My cousin Courtney who would visit me in just a few days was not texting me about the Beyoncé concert we were set to attend that weekend.

The message read: "Aunt Clarine said she wants you to care for the baby."

What the actual fuck is my life? was all I could think.

I didn't respond. I turned my phone off and cried into one of our many lovely, but unnecessary, throw pillows. Maybe if I just ignored the message it would go away?

Bennett was napping peacefully down the hall, we were approaching his second birthday, and honestly, I had zero interest in caring for another child. As we prepared for Bennett to turn two, I felt like we were entering a new chapter in our family's life. Our son would be attending school in the fall, Matt was headed back to work, and I felt like I finally had some breathing room. We were past the worst of the sleep regressions. I no longer had to pack basically a suitcase full of mostly necessary kid items every time we left the house, or fear that he was going to crawl into the dog's food or fall in the shower, which would result in an emergency room visit (both of these did indeed happen). Early motherhood was joyous, but at times it also felt smothering to me. It took two years for me to even begin to adjust to this new and immutable identity. Forever and ever, I will be Bennett's mother and it's the greatest gift, but also a life-altering experience. I was just starting to feel comfortable, and a bit more settled in this new identity, and now someone wanted me to take on another child. My whole being said no.

It sounds reasonable for me to say "No, thank you" to suddenly caring for someone else's newborn, but under the circumstances it felt horribly selfish.

My aunt was asking because my cousin, Imani Serafina Roberson, was missing. She had dinner at my aunt's house on Sunday, July sixteenth, and she had not been seen since. By the time the text message arrived, it had been six days, and we were fairly certain she had been killed by an abusive partner. Still, no arrests had been made and progress on her case was moving at a glacial pace. In the meantime, the aforementioned newborn was with his biological father, also known as the lead suspect in my cousin's killing. The entire situation was incomprehensible and impossible to process, especially since we were still very much in the thick of it. I always knew the world to be a dark and dangerous place, but this was next level.

Courtney and I were working arm in arm to support our aunt through this crisis, but I knew at some point my aunt would need to decide what to do about the baby. My aunt, a survivor who has been in abusive relationships, was now married and happy for over twenty years. She has seen and sustained more in her sixty-three years than most people will their entire lives. Unfortunately, if Imani was dead this would not be the first child my aunt lost. Prior to my cousin's disappearance, she had already lost three children, one just a few years ago to COVID, one to cancer, and one to gun violence. If we were right, Imani would be her fourth child to die, and her second child to die in less than three years. And of her remaining two children, one is incarcerated and the other has ALS. There was no question that my aunt deserved a respite.

I felt like a terrible, horrible, selfish person. Like I was failing not only my aunt but every other female relative who came before me and carried more with less. The women who were my childhood role models—my maternal grandmother and my mother, who would have literally given you the shirt off their backs. They had no time nor tolerance for people who were selfish, or lacking in generosity. When I was in third or fourth grade, one day we were driving home from church and there was a man on the side of the road with a sign asking for work in exchange for food. That wasn't something we saw regularly when driving around the Hudson Valley. My mother told my father to pull over and let the man know he would be right back. When we got to our house, without even taking her jacket off, she packed up our family's planned Crock-Pot dinner in old, empty tubs of Country Crock margarine, grabbed what cash she could find, plus snacks for kids, and sent my dad right back out the door. When he left, I asked her, "But what are we going to eat for dinner now?" The heat of her disappointment scalds me to this day. I learned a lesson that has been seared into my soul and I went to bed hungry that night.

That is how I was raised, so the idea of saying no to my aunt was horrendous. I did not want to let a woman down who had already lost so much. I always tell people to ask for help, that asking for help especially during periods of grief and trauma is how you survive, and now I was saying no to someone who was desperate for my help. Who was I to sit on my overpriced-throw-pillowed high horse? Everyone in my family knew that we could afford it. I sat around looking at our new house, my best-selling book on the shelves, the phone loaded with major contacts that could boost my already successful business to support another child—it was my responsibility to step up and provide for this child. If not me, who would?

At the same time, I had also watched my mother, my grandmother, and a bevy of aunties say yes to everyone but themselves. I often wondered if all of that doing for others contributed to my mother's death at just forty-nine, my maternal grandmother's heart attack in her early thirties, or my paternal grandmother's heart attack in her sixties and the many strokes that followed. What are the consequences of not putting ourselves and our needs first? I feared they might be too great for me to bear.

Nonetheless, the guilt was suffocating. After the tears, sweats, and erratic reaction to nap time being infiltrated with deep questions, I sat still and somewhere beneath all that guilt was a quiet insistence that I would not do it. That I should not do it. Somewhere beneath the layers of grit about *how* I could do it, I knew that saying no was the right choice. Not for my aunt. For me.

Even so, I struggled to say no. To say no to someone whose child was missing and likely dead, that I wouldn't take on one of the four children who've been left behind. There was no way not to feel like a piece of shit. The guilt that surfaces when you're a first-generation success witnessing the way the world treats your people, and having to accept that even if you can, it is not your role to fix it all, is a very special thing. Being Black in America is simply, truly exhausting. Every statistic you can think of—economic mobility and opportunity; health outcomes; educational attainment; home ownership—we are generally at or near the bottom of the pile, and when it comes to issues of safety and violence it gets even worse. Black Americans are twice as likely as white Americans to die from gun violence. Black women experience sexual assault at a disproportionate rate and one in five Black women are survivors of rape. We are tragically less safe and regularly left behind in this country.

But I knew that even with the material means, and my awareness of the racial safety gap that exists in America, I shouldn't do it, because *I* didn't have any remaining capacity. The help that you offer others must be aligned with your capacity and I had none, or next to none. I was tapped professionally and personally. I genuinely didn't feel like I could do it or like I was meant to do it. I held my stomach and closed my eyes and said a silent prayer just to make sure. And yes, while we may have had the means, that child was not for us.

When uncertainty arises, getting clear early on where you need to draw the line around your needs vis-à-vis the needs of others is crucial. Overloading your plate when life is already hard only makes things harder for you. Further, when you overdo, you keep others from doing the things that they are meant to do, no matter how hard those things may be. My aunt did not deserve any of this tragedy or pain, neither did the child, and neither did I. My privilege didn't mean my pain and trauma didn't matter because your pain and trauma always matter.

I was in a season where I needed to listen to myself and honor my boundaries, but it was still so hard to say no because I *could* have said yes. My no wasn't rooted in a lack of means, but a lack of emotional capacity and our individual, emotional capacity is something only we can assess.

The no wasn't about my professional demands making another child impossible. The no was not about our circumstances. The no was about me. It was about me listening to myself and what I believe is best for myself.

The sense of responsibility was overwhelming because I love my family, and I deeply believe in helping others. I've centered my life around Matthew 25:40: "Whatever you do for the least of these brothers of mine, you do for me."

As a Black woman, a childhood caretaker, and now a mom, putting the needs of others before my own comes naturally to me. As I assessed how to respond to my aunt, I realized that I hold an internal expectation that love must involve sacrifice.

But that's just not true. Good love shouldn't feel sacrificial. Sacrifice breeds resentment and, left to fester, infects love until it dies.

At its core good love doesn't mean always feeling good, but it should mean always feeling good about yourself. Good love, real love, requires boundaries, and they become even more essential during seasons of hardship and uncertainty. You have to know what your limits are if you want to live and love well when life gets hard. If not, your boundaries are unclear, and how will someone else be clear about what matters to you?

There were several weeks during the worst of my long COVID when I was too sick to work and I had to tell all my clients I was taking three weeks off. When I came back, I spoke to each of them individually about the new boundaries, boundaries that were rooted in love for myself first and foremost. I wanted to get back to my life and in order for me to do that, I needed to not sacrifice my health in that moment. At work that meant no more quick turnarounds, no more late-night emails, and no back-to-back calls. These were all things I was happy to do under normal circumstances but now were impossible to manage given my health challenges. I was met with understanding, mostly. In one case, my new boundaries simply did not align with a client's business objectives, and they gave me notice.

It was the first time I'd been fired. It hurt bad, but I knew I did the right thing for me. I would love to tell you I had no regrets, but it's not that simple. It hurt financially and had a very real impact on me and my family. Boundaries are almost never easy because they often require you to disappoint people, but they help us stay true to who we are and what we need.

Another child would have been a sacrifice too great for me to bear, so I said no, not only for myself, but for the child I already had. In order to be the best possible mother to Bennett, I need to be the best possible version of Marisa. I knew I was already hitting my limit emotionally as a new mom; it would be like throwing myself off a cliff without a parachute even though I truly loved my beautiful aunt and this innocent baby. Pain would have been to agree. The sacrifice would have bruised me.

When our backs are against the wall, it's tempting to think, *If I just keep going, keep pushing, keep asking myself for more, I will be all right.* No, you won't. As much as you may have danced around what you need to feel whole and good, you must stop because you're hurting yourself.

Cheryl Woods Giscombe developed a framework called the superwoman schema (SWS) based on the qualitative research to capture the direct connection between stress and health disparities among African American women, and I am confident this concept is applicable to everyone.

SWS often occurs when Black women have a perceived obligation to present an image of strength, an obligation to suppress emotions, resistance to being vulnerable or depending on others for help, motivation to succeed despite limited resources, and prioritization of caregiving over self-care. Some research suggests that women who experience these things can (but not in all cases) experience greater stress and depression. I was this woman in the past and I was not going to become her again.

My aunt's ask was driven by the love she had for the child. The love that she has always had for all of us. My no was also rooted in my love for her and all of us. There was no way for us to take on her grandson. This wasn't about sacrifice, this was about truth-telling. This was good love.

Good love is saying no when you know that's the right answer even if it causes you or someone else pain. Good love is about being honest about whatever our needs are and accommodating them. At times, it is deeply uncomfortable, but we have to put ourselves first if we are going to be of any real use to someone else. We hear it all the time, but in practice it is so very hard, especially if you are going to disappoint someone you love. Whenever I think about saying no and being compassionate to myself, and I fear disappointing someone else, I ask myself, *If this were Allison instead of you, what would you tell her to do?* Allison is my childhood best friend and I only want the very best for her. It is much easier for me to swap myself for someone else in order to give me permission to take what I need or say no to someone. This kind of love, that isn't rooted in sacrifice but first and foremost in compassion and care, has been a lifelong struggle for me and I manage it by inserting someone else into my place. It makes it easier to act on my own behalf. Nothing about this is easy. Even if our inclination to say yes comes from a good place and not a childhood trauma, there needs to be room for no. That space between what you can and cannot give is only accessible to you. It is the place where you take a deep look at what matters to you before you can give to others. When we choose what's truly best for us, we honor ourselves. Isn't that what those who truly love you would want you to do?

And you know what? My aunt understood. She didn't push or try to manipulate, convince, or cajole.

She knew I would continue to do everything I could to support her, and that was enough for her.

In your case, you may be manipulated or cajoled. Someone may push you, or family may consider you uppity or someone who thinks they are better than everyone else. Not every no is easily accepted even by those who love us, but if your no is rooted in honesty and compassion for yourself and love for others, then it is always the right answer.

I was relieved, and I made a promise to myself: I would find my cousin. Before Imani disappeared, everything I knew about missing person's cases came from Netflix shows, but I know how to get shit done. In that moment, I leveraged every resource at my disposal. I went full-on Olivia Pope. I called on my network of national and local leaders, celebrities, politicians, and media operatives and we launched a PR and public engagement campaign to find my cousin. In a matter of days, we created a website and a GoFundMe page, designed press kits and graphics for social media, and hosted a press conference. My aunt was on *Good Morning America*, *ABC World News Tonight*, and Stacey Abrams's office was calling on local investigators to get their thumbs out of their asses and find my cousin. We launched our campaign on Sunday, July thirtieth, and by Friday, August fourth, Imani's body was found, and her husband was arrested for murder. His trial is set to take place after this book is completed. If I had said yes to caring for her son, if I hadn't set that boundary I never would have had the energy to launch a nationwide search to find Imani.

This life is all about choices and my aunt now believes it was the right choice for that child too. My aunt told me how proud she was of me and Matt and what a good job we were doing caring for and loving Bennett. In our love and care she saw not just us, but my mother, her big sister. She saw her mother, my grandmother, reflected in our parenting, and she wanted this child to experience that as well, but now he is exactly where he belongs, with my aunt and her husband. Caring for him has been a truly joyful and healing experience for her. Labor intensive for sure, but full of happiness and hope as well. His presence after so much sorrow has been like a tiny ray of light that pokes through after storm clouds dissipate. His sweetness has made it easier for her to bear the bitter pain of grief.

Good love involves boundaries and self-compassion. We can't give and give and give until we break, but when we stop, healing is possible.

8

Flake...

It's OK to flake.

I realize that is a highly unpopular opinion, and you are probably wondering if I have any friends—I do—but it is the truth. Sometimes, it is OK to flake. Certain life events require so much of us that we simply do not have capacity for much else. It isn't just about setting boundaries; it is more about maintaining an ongoing awareness that you are under assault. Whatever has transpired in your life has made you more unreliable simply by nature of the problem being all-consuming. Like it or not, an ongoing period of uncertainty will alter who you are as a person. Fundamentally you just don't have as much space when you are managing new and unfamiliar and often painful territory. Whether you want it to be true or not, a sick parent, a pending divorce, financial uncertainty as you navigate having your job eliminated by your employer's use of AI, global instability, it all takes a toll. Focusing on one big important thing means there is less room for you to focus on other things, no matter how important they are. You will disappoint people, you will fail at things, and you will drop some balls. Therefore, during difficult or uncertain times, expectations should fly out the window and be replaced with grace.

Grace requires us to accept that life or a situation is different from the way it was before uncertainty entered the room. Your life is now less predictable, in many cases more tiresome, tumultuous, and heavy. Older, previous ways of moving through the world all need to be evaluated through this new lens. Your life is now like one of those snow globes that moms and grandmas would have placed on precious white doilies, so you knew not to mess with them. Except it doesn't feel delicate or precious. You are existing inside that snow globe right after your younger sister shakes it so hard she nearly breaks it. You are overwhelmed inside an unseeing mess, and you need to figure out how to live in this season.

Let the season change you.

When uncertainty enters the room, you need to figure out which responsibilities you can flake on and which you cannot, as quickly as possible. It is the only way you will ever sort through the mess and ensure you are taking care of the things that matter most. Those items that are truly precious have to be uncovered in order for you to figure out what to do and how to manage your life. Think of it like you're in the middle of a move. You're just beginning to unpack the mountain of boxes delivered to your new home. You need to prioritize. Not everything needs to be unpacked today (unless you're my husband), but some things definitely do. You walk around and read the labels on the boxes to determine what is most important in the midst of this mess. You need underwear, you need plates to eat off, you need your toddler's lovey or else you're driving straight toward a bedtime crisis. You don't need the family photos, or as much as I love them, your books when you first start unpacking; those things can literally sit in a box for weeks without it being a problem. Think of your life in this way. Everything is a mess, but not everything bears the same level of importance.

Determining what matters most and what can be put off, or what should be dropped all together, requires you to pause and honestly evaluate everything that is on your plate. If you are a parent, you cannot stop caring for your child, but you can teach them how to help out around the house more so you can do less overall. You need to clear the decks as much as possible to accommodate whatever has taken over your life. At this time, this version of you must insist on change. You "manage it all" by not managing it all. You learn to say "no" or "no, thank you" or "not right now."

And when it is a commitment that's already been made, you need to be particularly discerning. Only you can determine whether a prior commitment is something you can flake on, or if it is too precious to ignore. And it often will not be particularly straightforward; depending on what you are navigating in your period of uncertainty your answers may change over time, so on an ongoing basis you have to assess your capacity vis-à-vis whatever it is you are managing and then decide from there what else you can or cannot add to your plate. It requires intentionality, discernment, and clarity in regard to both your values and your priorities.

As anyone who's been there knows, who lives, who dies, when they die, how they die, how long it takes—one of the most important parts of our existence, our death—is generally largely beyond human control. In the fall of 2023, after losing my cousin, we were still preparing for the death of my mother-in-law, Marcia. By then she had been sick for over a year, at "death's door" for most of that period, and it was absolutely brutal.

Watching Marcia die slowly from a distance was a reminder of the enormity, the true volume and potential for human suffering that exists in the ordinary business of living and dying in this world. While she was dying, in the midst of the heaviness from all that grief, I was scheduled to lead a grief retreat in rural North Carolina. That's right, I was meant to be off helping others navigate their grief in the middle of a period of tremendous personal and family grief. If you're wondering, *What was she thinking? That sounds like a terrible idea*, you would be absolutely right. But I made a commitment to do it, and I had every intention of following through on that promise.

The agreement had been in place for nearly a year and people who I didn't even know were spending their hard-earned money to have me talk to them about grief and living with loss. That meant the world to me. But I failed to recognize that this season of grief I was experiencing had changed me. I was carrying too much already to be counted on firmly for anything more. My normal life and expectations had to be put on pause. And this was not the same as my cousin's baby. This wasn't a weighty, long-term commitment to care for another human, it was a weekend-long retreat, so I thought I would be fine. But honestly, I barely had room for my own grief and my husband's, how was I to hold space for an entire cohort of people's grief? I was operating on autopilot, and never paused to ask the question, *Do I even have capacity for this?* Thankfully, someone else asked it instead.

It was my friend Lizzie, who is a clinical psychologist, who spoke up and questioned my plans. She asked in her kind and gentle manner, "Are you sure you still want to do this retreat?" I was exhausted. And I knew right away the answer was no. I was not capable. I was not in a season where I could pour into others. I was scared to be so far away from home, two hours' drive to and from the airport on both ends with limited flight options. If my mother-in-law died while I was gone it would take me longer to get home from Boone, North Carolina, than it would have from London or Paris. How the fuck did I ever think I was going to be able to do this retreat?

Well, I believed I could do it because that is what I do. I have been showing up for and supporting others during times of grief and uncertainty since I was a child and my mother first got sick. The people who registered for my retreat needed help and they believed I could provide it. Even with everything I know about grief, the thought never once entered my mind that I wasn't capable.

What I failed to remember is that when we are in prolonged periods of pain and uncertainty those stressors change who we are. Our physical and mental capabilities have been altered by the situation.

Stress associated with loss activates the hypothalamic-pituitary-adrenal axis, which releases cortisol (a stress hormone). Especially in the early phases of loss and grief, elevated cortisol levels often lead to sleep disturbances, appetite changes, immune suppression, and even cardiovascular strain. Other research has shown that this stress reaction is associated with cognitive changes including difficulty concentrating, memory disturbances, and disruptions in executive functions like planning and decision-making. These are neurological responses to emotional trauma and loss. Like it or not, you are different, because your brain and body are adaptively dealing with emotional trauma by focusing resources to deal with the stressor at hand. This might show up as forgetfulness, exhaustion, physical pain, or irritability, and is not a sign of weakness, but that you are dealing with something threatening and painful. An extrovert may retreat into themselves more, an introvert might require more community, a person who everyone always counts on may become a flake.

Whether because you are a caretaker or you are in a period of anticipatory grief, illness, or other circumstantial loss, whatever it is you cannot count on yourself in the same ways. You must decide to stop, to say not right now. You have to adapt, prioritize, and reconsider your expectations of yourself.

During hard times, stop and pause to ask yourself, *What do I need to be OK right now?*

I knew what was most important: supporting my husband as he prepared to lose his mother. What I didn't do is take that a step further and ask, *What do I need to do? What do I need to let go of in order to support Matt effectively?* I allowed myself to be limited by my own beliefs about myself, my work, and my commitment to serving others. But what I didn't understand was that in this season, all I could actually do was support myself and my family and, no one else matters to me as much as Matt and Bennett.

I was just too buried under the day-to-day demands of survival to recognize that I was living in a time where my circumstances conflicted with my identity. This was not a time for powering through, this was a time for slowing down and drawing very clear boundaries around the needs of myself and my family.

In asking the question, Lizzie removed a twenty-pound weight I didn't even realize was sitting on my chest. My mind suddenly opened up to the possibility of not doing this thing I'd committed to a year prior. I realized in my conversation with Lizzie, and a conversation with another friend who also pushed me to cancel, that I was scared to lead the retreat. I was emotionally excavated. I was something beyond empty. My heart felt like it had been scraped clean.

There was simply nothing left. I was in a period of familial darkness. Inside of our home it felt like we were waiting out a storm. I was on autopilot moving forward with something simply because I am someone who believes in following through on a commitment. This is who I've always been, but in that season, I simply could not be that person, and I needed to accept that.

By the time I had that conversation with her, the retreat was only three weeks away. I needed to make a decision quickly. I knew in my bones she was right. As much as I value commitment, I value excellence more.

I was nervous reaching out to the folks who'd hired me. I've mostly been lucky and generally have been met with kindness during seasons of grief, but I know that isn't how it always goes.

A few months before my mother's death, while working full-time, managing my mother's affairs, and running a charity, an organization reached out to me. They had a similar name to our cheekily named charity, Saving Second Base, which I'd started with friends when I was twenty-four years old to raise money for breast cancer research and direct care services from young professionals. We believed that if we began supporting breast cancer research at a young age, by the time we were middle-aged the disease would be eradicated. The other organization was a T-shirt company based in Philly. They made shirts with baseballs over the boobs that people wore for breast cancer charity walks and such. Right after my mother died, I'd invited this organization to our annual fund-raising gala in New York City. I thought we could collaborate with them and raise money together to fight this horrible disease. Six weeks after my mother's death, which they were informed of in my outreach, they served me with a cease-and-desist order and a copyright infringement lawsuit. I was twenty-five, with a recently deceased mother, running a tiny all-volunteer cancer charity out of the basement of the investment bank where I worked, and they came after me. They didn't care about my pain, or my desire for friendship and collaboration.

From that experience I learned that grief and uncertainty aren't always met with compassion and empathy, but at times it's met with indifference and other times downright nastiness. As I prepared for the call with the retreat company, I reviewed my contract and legally approved talking points. I wiped my sweaty palms on my yoga pants as I spoke to the retreat organizer. Her words, "I was wondering how you were still going to do this. I completely understand. We will make a plan for cancellation. It's OK," so shocked me that of course I started to cry. I knew I'd made the right call, and her kindness only validated my decision.

When you find yourself in a similar situation,

please get rid of anything that does not serve you, support you, or bring you joy. Period. Everything else can wait, and the people you flake on, who love you, will forgive you. You can even preemptively apologize to them now. You will need them, so be good to your friends, but whatever your personal crisis is, that is what needs you more right now. You need to create as much space as possible for the rest of your life to be peaceful in order to offset the overwhelming tide of uncertainty. What is truly meant for you will still be meant for you when the waves recede.

In doing what was truly best for me and saying, "I cannot do this right now," I was free to do what I was meant to do: be there for Matt. I will always be grateful that I had enough sense to listen to my friend, because of course the day Marcia passed away, I would have been in Boone, North Carolina, had I maintained my commitment to that retreat. Thanks to Lizzie and the compassion of the retreat organizers, I was right where I belonged that day, with Matt. I want you to remember that periods of uncertainty require us to have different priorities and that is not just OK, it should be expected.

When you're in a period where life is a mess and you're mired in pain, you have to give yourself permission to alter your way of living and being in the world. I gave myself permission to have all the feelings, to go to therapy, to engage in longer workouts, and rest more when and where I could. But I failed to give myself permission to stop being me professionally, to press pause on who I think I need to be, to flake, to drop the ball, to be more unreliable. In my case, I needed to get off the hamster wheel of high expectations that I've been on pretty much all my life. I needed to let myself "flake."

9

...Help

IN ORDER FOR you to absorb and manage the experience, you need to first figure out the impact of uncertainty on your life.

If the impact will be enormous, please get clear that you can't do it by yourself. Some people are raised in environments where you couldn't ask for help, and therefore it can be very hard to feel safe doing so. Research has shown that individuals who experience a high burden of stress, adversity, and neglect in childhood often struggle to seek help in adulthood. Early experiences of neglect, or being left alone, can make it hard in later life to even perceive social support or help from others, because it isn't part of how you were made to be. Your environment was not predictable or responsive to your needs, and seeking help was simply not a skill you learned.

Asking for help is hard, so hard. It requires you to expose yourself. How can you possibly trust that someone will actually show up for you if you've never had that happen for you before?

This is no easy task, so try to start small. You have to commit to finding a way to believe that people are better than what you've experienced so far. Test them out by asking for help with something that would add value to your life right now, but perhaps isn't the most essential thing. We build trust with others by giving them a chance to prove themselves. Do not let a poor prior experience, or even your trauma, shape your entire perspective of the world and what's possible within it. Because you couldn't rely on some people, perhaps even some essential people, doesn't mean you can't rely on anyone ever.

Hyper-independence is worshipped in our society, and in a society that worships independence and self-reliance to such a degree, asking for help often comes with feelings of shame. You may hear yourself saying, "I feel bad…" You may feel like a failure asking for help. You must be doing something wrong if you need help. Nope, you aren't. Humans evolved in community for a reason. We are meant to help one another, and yet asking makes us cringe.

There is a vulnerability required to present your needs to others, to the world, and just hope that someone answers the call. I love to help people, but for a long time, I hated to ask for help. I simply do not want to be reliant on other humans. It is too intimate and makes me feel far too exposed. It feels like you're standing naked in a room full of strangers. What if they say no? The idea that you might be rejected when you are at your most vulnerable is devastating, but we find our people and build deep community when we ask for and accept help, so we have to try.

Mutual dependency and reliance on another human being feel like weakness. I wonder if they will reject me. I contemplate how much they already have on their plate and the thought of inconveniencing them makes me sick. And in some cases, with close family and friends I think, *If they really wanted to help me, they would just help. I shouldn't have to ask.*

In our hypercompetitive, deeply individualistic culture we all usually need much more help than we realize or are comfortable admitting. Even when life isn't hard, we could use more help, but that admittance often feels like being judged, failure, or seeming "too much." When those thoughts arise in you, I want you to channel the last time you helped someone else and how good that felt to you. Did you judge them for asking for your support, or were you glad they asked and grateful to be able show up? This idea that if we don't do it all we are doing it wrong, is simply wrong.

Alloparenting is a weird word that means a number of different "parental-type figures" help care for children than just the standard two parents of a nuclear family.

In our country we have evolved away from aunties and uncles and godparents and grandparents being intimately involved in the care of our children. My dear friend Liza has seven kids (yes she is quite special), and she also lives next door to her brother and sister-in-law who have five children. We spent New Year's Eve with them and as I watched my son run wild tended to by older children, everyone from both houses made food, organized a massive party, and generally contributed to the joy and chaos of the household I was full-on jealous.

Like children, you need support. Growth does not mean that you stop falling down; it means you always find a way to get back up and sometimes that is with the help of someone else's hand.

Life gets hard. The first signs you need support are usually emotional. Then they become physical. Studies have shown that repressing or ignoring our needs can even elevate risk for serious conditions such as cardiovascular disease. If you're constantly feeling stressed, depressed, anxious, or overwhelmed you are probably in need of some form of assistance. If you can't shake the stomachache, headache, or insomnia, those are also often signs as well. Help isn't just a practical matter either. Social support you experience can be healing. There is research showing that both social support and social integration, that feeling of really being a part of a community, can lead to faster illness recovery. Asking for help is a form of medicine.

In asking for help we extend mercy to ourselves. When we fail to ask for help when it is desperately needed, we cause more pain. Our pride and our ego can sometimes prevent us from having the strength to ask for the help we need.

During my bout with long COVID, Beyoncé announced her Cowboy Carter concert. I was determined to go and secured six tickets for me and my friends. The day of the concert the weather was terrible—in the fifties and raining—and I was super worried for my health, so I asked another friend, Emily, for help securing indoor seats and she miraculously succeeded moments before the show was set to begin. I was so proud of myself for advocating for Marisa and asking for what I needed, but my ego kept me from asking for everything I needed, namely a wheelchair. As much as I'd evolved in my thinking around illness and disability, the idea of needing a wheelchair to go see Beyoncé perform was honestly too emotionally painful because of my own stubbornness and pride. So instead of renting one for the day, I spent about an hour on my feet before the show, probably another hour during (because it's Beyoncé and I couldn't help it), and then we walked nearly a mile to our ride at the end of the show. I was physically destroyed all because my pride kept me from asking for the help I needed. Turns out, I am very capable of being a fool.

When uncertainty arises the onus is on each of us to determine what we need, as I mentioned earlier, drop our ego, and ask for help. This is where I usually take off my writer-creator hat and put on my strategist hat. I will ask myself honestly, *Where am I feeling stress, tension, or experiencing roadblocks? What am I doing that is making this situation harder? How might others help me—free or paid? Who can I ask for help and with what activities?*

During the worst of my illness, it was an evolving situation with symptoms that would regularly shift or change, and I knew I couldn't manage it all on my own. So I got my aforementioned childhood best friend Allison to serve as my operations manager at work so I wouldn't drop as many balls. She also took on various "mom" tasks I wouldn't have felt comfortable outsourcing to anyone else, like making Bennett a dentist appointment or researching summer camps.

I later asked my dad's best friend Kenny to start making us dinner once a week, which was happily my role in our house, and with Matt's work schedule it was impossible for him to take this on. Kenny became a support person in that regard. It wasn't easy for me to give up my role as family chef because cooking brings me joy, but when it started to cause pain, I had to step away. You want to ask for help before it's physically painful.

At another point, when my legs were incredibly weak and it became difficult to stand in the shower, I asked my friend Carmella, who is a hairdresser, to wash my hair for me. Anything I could remove from my plate was appreciated because I needed all the help I could get.

Spoon theory states that when your body is weak and you only have so much energy to allocate in a given day, that energy is represented by spoons. You visualize the number of spoons you think you have for the day. It helps you think more practically about what is possible. Some days I had only four spoons and one spoon might be allocated to Bennett's morning routine, one for his bedtime routine, leaving me with two spoons. If I took a shower instead of a bath, that would be one more spoon gone. It was devastating, but it helped me quantify my energy, figure out what I was going to do with it and then ask for help with the rest. It is a theory commonly utilized by people who manage disabilities or chronic illnesses, but I believe it can be applied to anyone navigating grief, pain, stress, or uncertainty. We all need help with energy and prioritization when life becomes challenging.

Life can be very lonely. Uncertainty can feel like you're on an island, all alone, out to sea, at night. No one can fully understand your experience, and you often feel something beyond lost: unmoored. Help should not just be in the practical and tactical things you do but also consider the social and emotional side. If it isn't physical, no one sees your pain, and sometimes even when it is physical, if you're not bald from chemo or walking with a cane, people may think it's not that bad. They will assume you are fine, and they will only know you aren't if you ask for help. Psychological and emotional help is saying, "I need help." You don't need to have it all figured out with master plans and spreadsheets like you're a commander in some war zone. The unloading of three words—"I need help"—is sometimes the most important to get clear in finding help. Let the person or people on the other end help you with deciding what exactly that means, because you may not even know what you need! All you know is that things are not right. That you are stuck, or bothered, or in pain. You are suffering. It doesn't take a million therapy sessions, and you don't need to worry about who to say it to. Just make sure you say it out loud to someone who is listening, who you trust, who may not be in your same position but is a caring individual or community of people.

I have my eleven roommates from college—we do not see each other every day (I wish) and there's no *Sex in the City* vibes, at least not anymore, but I know that if I am able to say it out loud, they will collectively get to work. When my mother-in-law was dying they showed up and showed me love by providing long-distance emotional support. I often hid, crying in hotel stairwells texting them furiously from Green Bay over some big feeling or something that went wrong, or some trauma revisited. They were always there. When shit goes down they will send food, gifts, thoughtful cards, or silly memes. They will do research and check in on a set schedule to see how I'm doing. They may fly across the world, or they may stay up late helping me figure it out. And when one of them is in trouble, I am expected, and honored, to do the same. This is what mutual aid looks like and how community is meant to work. Let go of the shame and start with those three words, *I need help*, and see who answers the call. Anyone can do that. I know you have roots—it may not be in your DNA, not how you were taught, those words may not have existed before today in your vocabulary, but they do now.

Asking for proper help can ensure your heart survives. It can save you from a crisis. Otherwise, all you'll be is battered and bruised, negatively changed and unsure, but asking for help will allow you to emerge from this season of uncertainty free from bitterness and resentment because help makes us feel loved.

When we let our guard down, ask for help, and are supported, it opens up a new window of possibility while we're in the fog. It shows us a vision—that we can do it, as long as we ask for what we need. Through the love and care of others we are buoyed.

Accepting the help requires us to humble ourselves. It requires us to say, "I cannot do all of this on my own. I am not deficient, I am not a failure, but I do need help in order to live well." There is strength in that kind of humility. But also when someone offers you help, please accept it without guilt or shame or embarrassment. Matt would often offer to help me with something in the kitchen and I would insist I was fine. I didn't want to "bother" him when in actuality I needed someone to get me out of the kitchen and into our bed. What I wish I had the strength to say instead is, "I am struggling, I know this is hard for you, too, that I can't finish Bennett's breakfast, but I cannot be on my feet right now." It's not like he was going to get mad at me for saying something like that, I just felt guilty for adding to his existing burden. He went from having a wife who typically moved at 150 miles per hour to having one who moves at a snail's pace. I didn't want to make things worse for him by being needy, but "clear is kind." I would have made his life easier by being more direct about my needs and we would have found a way to manage them together.

We must learn that not asking for help is rooted in assumptions. You are clairvoyant or a mind reader based on past pains and experiences. You were rejected once before and have resolved to act alone. Or perhaps you think altruistically, that by doing it all alone you are doing someone else a favor, but we know little about one another's internal lives and struggles. Maybe someone you're about to call on really wants you to ask.

When you are struggling to navigate something challenging, foreign, and uncertain, if there is no playbook for you, then there certainly does not exist a playbook for those who want to show up and help. We cannot be angry with someone for not helping if we haven't asked for their help. And if someone hasn't offered help that does not mean they don't love us; they probably just don't know what to do, or perhaps they aren't aware you need their help. Help them help you, by asking for what you need.

The refusal to ask for what we need is so often rooted in assumptions that are usually more about us than them. It is about our own insecurities and the questioning of what we truly deserve. But don't we all deserve to live with as much ease as possible when life gets impossibly hard? Yes.

Your muscle for accepting help comes from self-love. You must love and believe in yourself in order to deem yourself worthy of care and assistance, especially if it's ongoing. You have to see your value in order to even ask. A lot of us don't really, truly love ourselves enough. We believe all the love in our hearts is on reserve for others and instead of speaking to ourselves with love, we are usually our worst critics. We are fully capable of playing superwoman when it comes to our loved ones, but we keep our heads down when it comes to our own needs. But there is a better way for you.

You need community. I know you may not have eleven very helpful and supportive roommates from college. I can hear you complaining about your lack of community and what has warranted it: access, location, situational setbacks, loss, et cetera, but you must view building the community you deserve as a part of your healing process. You deserve mutual aid and reliance. You are not meant to do this life alone. Do the work and when your period of uncertainty is over, get ready to give.

You cannot experience genuine community if you don't believe others love you enough to want to help you. Love wants to help. It wants us to take care of our people and be taken care of by them. To make them feel appreciated, supported, nurtured, provided for, and vice versa. When people love you and you are in pain, all anyone will want to do is fix it. They may not be able to fix it or make it disappear, but the question you have to ask yourself is, *Do I love and value myself enough to accept help from someone else?* And if not, how are you going to get there, so you don't have to do all this alone?

When asking for help, be specific, direct, and clear with folks. This will reduce the likelihood you will be disappointed. People are busy, and even if they want to help you, it is something they will have to fit into their lives, so be crystal clear on what you need and when you need it. Also, be prepared to be flexible. Not everyone is going to do things exactly the way you would when they do something to help you. For instance, when I was sick I obviously needed all the help I could get with my son. My father is the best Pop-Pop and loves Bennett very much. He is also late for basically everything. He may have even been late for his own birth. He took Bennett one day so I could rest and Matt could work, and he brought him home far too late for his nap. Of course I am one of those controlling people who sleep trained early and maintained those habits throughout, so I was not pleased to receive a tired and cranky toddler. But at the end of the day it was definitely better than Bennett jumping on me all day while I battled a mind-crushing headache. In situations like these, I like to apply something my therapist calls the rule of six. Will this thing that is annoying today (cranky toddler) still be a problem in six hours, six days, six weeks, or six months? The answer is usually no, so release some control and be OK with things not being just so but still getting done. Do not let the perfect be the enemy of the good.

We all know that some people won't show up for us the way we expect them to. Love is to show them some grace. If someone hurts you by their inaction or lack of response when you ask for help, allow yourself a moment to assess the situation. Is this their usual behavior? If so, why did you choose to ask them? You were digging a grave. Or are they usually great at showing up for you? If so, they could have something challenging going on in their life that has put them at capacity. Or you know what, maybe they aren't at capacity and just can't. That's not the person to help you this time. Maybe next time. People miss messages, they flake and disappoint us in times of need, but it often doesn't mean they don't love us. They could be afraid, avoidant, or overwhelmed. Try to avoid jumping to any conclusions and becoming resentful.

Only you can decide if this person is worthy of your grace, or if this is someone who you need to move on from. Not everyone is capable of loving you the way you need and deserve to be loved.

Just remember that help is about love. Giving and receiving what we deserve when we need it most and it starts with you. Self-love is the foundation for receiving love from others.

10

Perform...

CULTURE IS EVERYTHING. Culture shows us the rules without telling us the rules. Culture: the values, norms, and expectations of any group of people tell us what matters to them. It is the foundation that determines what is and what is not acceptable, what feelings are appropriate, and which ones should be hidden, and so on. Our culture, whether the one we create within our homes or the one in which we engage in the world shows us how to behave. Culture often also provides us with a sense of direction in terms of how we should show up in the world. We are conditioned by our culture to play certain roles in certain ways in our society. Every title we carry—wife, business executive, father, middle child—our culture holds expectations for how you are meant to perform your role.

There are cultures that are created for us as well as cultures that we create for ourselves. Some years ago, when Matt and I were still childless, I remember a friend sharing that their family—she has two little boys—has a set of core values that they repeat over and over to their children to help guide how they should show up in the world. It provides a framework for how they should treat themselves and others. I decided whenever we were fortunate enough to start a family we would do the same. Almost every day, I remind Bennett that he is "smart, kind, helpful, and brave." The culture Matt and I seek to create in our home is one of love, care, and support not just for one another, but for others out in the world. This is a culture we get to create for us, for Bennett.

When we all think back to our family of origin there was a culture there too. It may have been loving and supportive, a place where you felt seen, heard, and nurtured to your fullest potential, or there may be a degree of tension surrounding the home you were raised in and the culture you are building for your own home as an adult. My family is originally from a small town in Georgia called Statesboro. Every other summer, my parents spent their meager savings on a trip "down South" for the annual family reunion. In my childhood home, my mom was the boss. She was kind and humble about it and she ran our house impeccably well even after she got sick. Make no mistake, everyone knew Lisa was in charge of all of us, except down South. I have this very distinct memory of my mother grumbling to my aunt Kathy as she made my father a plate of food, not because she didn't want to, or didn't often do that at home, but she was angry about the cultural expectation that as a wife, as a woman, it was her job to keep my father fed. I don't know if she realized it during her lifetime, but she was definitely a feminist and she was not having that plate making. As another example, in traditional Western white American culture, we are made to believe that emotional expression, particularly the unrestrained type—women mourning in the streets, loud wailing, people crying out in anger or pain—is unseemly and generally ill advised in our public spaces. Somewhere between toddlerhood and adulthood, we learned to hide and suppress our feelings in the name of being appropriate and polite adults. We do it because it is what the culture demands, but what about our emotional maturity, or our mental health? It is not possible to live well with grief, pain, or uncertainty if you never openly express your feelings. You cannot hide your true self behind a mask of any kind because of cultural expectations or anything else. Doing so will greatly impede your ability to move with freedom and manage whatever life has thrown your way. You need to create a culture of care, take off your mask, and stop performing whatever culturally dictated role you've taken on, so you can get real about what you need to survive your time of grief and uncertainty.

Oftentimes, we do not even realize that we are performing.

In the literal middle of nowhere in Greece, I found myself in the back of a Sprinter van, alternating between quietly crying and cracking jokes in an attempt to lessen the seriousness of my situation. I was scared and embarrassed because I could barely breathe and it hurt to hold my head upright, but I couldn't seem to stop laughing and making light of the situation. I hate making people uncomfortable with my own discomfort. For me it feels deeply exposing and culturally unacceptable to be a Black woman who people take seriously; I believe it is my job to keep it together. As my grandmother used to say, "Ain't no use complaining 'cause don't no one wanna hear it anyway." I view it as my job, no matter what, to simply keep it moving, even when I shouldn't, even though I know better. So instead of keeping my mouth shut and protecting my lungs, I treated the ride like I was in my own personal all-female version of *The Hangover.* Instead of heading to Vegas for gambling and drugs, we were headed to the pulmonologist on the dark highways of Chalkidiki. We even picked up an inhaler on the way. All four of us in the van had mothers who died young after lengthy battles with a variety of chronic illnesses, and I was a visiting fellow teaching a course on writing about grief. I was finally doing my retreat, and I was so excited, except for the not-breathing part. I knew I was unwell, but I figured it was just the heat exacerbating my condition. I was sick and I knew I needed rest, but I wasn't especially concerned. After hours teaching in the sun, I went from taking photos of us on a beautiful cul-de-sac rooftop and shopping to fully losing my breath by dinner before the branzino was served. What felt like an inconvenience earlier in the day quickly morphed into a crisis with the cerulean Aegean Sea sparkling in the background. I couldn't deal with any of that, so instead, I made them promise to take lots of photos at the doctor's office because the entire thing was so absurd. I also told them I hoped, since all of them were single, that the doctor would be brilliant and hot, 'cause why not? I insisted this experience would wind up in a feature film or scripted series one day.

As sick and scared as I was I couldn't stop hiding my real feelings; the biggest of all was fear. It was an overwhelming amount of fear. The kind of fear that sits in your chest and weighs you down, which was not helpful given my breathing challenges. I couldn't stop acting like everything was OK, like I was OK.

If I could joke about it, I must be OK. I could not admit I was terrified, because I wasn't in a position of safety. I masked my fear, and I performed.

I cracked jokes and laughed my face off at my own mother's funeral. I spent years telling people "It's OK" when they said, "I'm sorry your mom died." I hosted nine of my roommates from college for our annual reunion a few weeks after my devastating pregnancy loss. This is what I do. I reach for joy and distraction and I perform. I am quite good at all of it. It is human nature to perform. Performance becomes a problem when we do it solely out of fear.

There is something in our culture that makes fear show up as weakness. Our commitment to independence and strength has created a society that undervalues the acknowledgment of real fear and sadness. Admitting you are afraid means you are weak and if you are already weak by virtue of race, gender, class, or sexual orientation, why would you ever admit you're afraid? But when uncertainty and overwhelming stress arrive we need to find a way to remove the various masks we reach for, to stop performing.

If you have always been the person taking care of everyone and everything no matter what, you have to stop performing that role. Take some time off. Retire the role all together. Do whatever you need to be flexible when uncertainty shows up. Performance can trap you. It's rigid, you've played this role many times before. You've mastered it so well, at times you can't tell who you really are from the performance. When performing, it's not natural to know that you are. In the fog of uncertainty, it may only be seen in hindsight. Did you have to attend the party? Did you have to give more? Why are you feeling so drained?

I am begging you: Do not remain committed to a role that doesn't directly serve, support, or help you.

If this is you, it may sound pretty—people tend to call it the classic Eldest Daughter, Star Soccer Mom, Most Valuable Employee. These are masks, because any role you're trapped in actually is a weakness.

We often reach for our masks when we feel insecure. A certain role is more culturally acceptable than our most authentic and natural selves. Maybe you've been told your whole life that you talk too much and that's now led to you rarely speaking up at work. Or perhaps you become a doctor like your parent, even though you feel drawn to the arts. Or perhaps you've stayed in an unhappy relationship because you don't want to be the only one in your friend group who is single. Culture dictates acceptability.

Back when I was working on Wall Street in the early 2000s, I was often the youngest, the only woman, and the only person of any color in the room. I knew this would be the case at an old-school, white-shoe firm that included in-house ushers. I loved them, but I still don't know why they were there. I decided I would own the place, and I played my part. I was going to be the Super Fun and Super Competent Black Girl with the hardest and most intense portfolio of clients. That was what I wanted, and it is what I built by performing and dressing the part. The tightest pencil skirts, the crispest blouses, super high heels, and then, and this is where it gets pretty weird, I added glasses. I absolutely 100 percent did not need the glasses, but I wore them to meetings with partners. I decided the glasses and straightened hair made me appear most competent as the Solo Black Girl Badass Banker so that's how I rolled. We often choose to perform when we feel inadequate. When we enter into a space or culture that we feel does not accept us. I was an outsider, first person in my working-class family to go to a four-year college, and I was Black. I felt I had something to compensate for, so I created the part that I felt was expected of me and I played it to perfection.

Insecurity means "not firmly fixed; liable to give way or break." If you're performing, this is where you are: at a breaking point. Somehow you have been destabilized and there is often an overwhelming amount of fear that has followed. Fear of death, or financial security, or some worsening health challenge, or perhaps political instability. It is all destabilizing. It can feel easiest to simply stick to the script, to keep playing the roles you are most familiar with, because there is a perceived sense of safety in familiarity.

"Is this role serving me?" When you are at the family picnic, and the family is expecting you to do the grilling, salad-making, and cleaning up after the aunties yet again this year, but you are actually really tired, I want you to pause and ask yourself this: *Is this the part I am really meant to play right now? Does playing this role contribute to my self-care and well-being?*

Sometimes even if we love a role we play, we need a break from it. There are bigger examples of that picnic where you are doing the same. Because even our chosen roles, the areas where we aren't necessarily, actively performing have folded into this need to accommodate whatever has taken over our life.

Before finding myself in the back of a Sprinter van in Greece, I was playing a part I'd been rehearsing for years, Best-selling Author. I was leading a writing retreat focused on grief in an idyllic location. This was a part that I wanted, desperately, especially after having to cancel my grief retreat the year before. I had arrived in Thessaloniki, Greece, six days earlier with a heart full of hope. Helping people acknowledge, accept, and find their own unique way to live with loss is one of the things I excel at and love to do. It was all very genuine and authentic. This was not a performance but a role I was built for and genuinely wanted to play, but it became a performance because I was hiding the gravity of my illness when it was time to pay attention to myself. What I wanted to do as a teacher and author was out of alignment because of how unwell I was. I simply was not up to the task in the ways I'd envisioned or planned for, and I refused to accept that reality.

When we continue to perform a role that no longer fits due to a change in our circumstances, we cause harm. At a minimum we make our circumstances, lives, and sometimes health worse when we simply keep performing without accommodating our physical or emotional needs. At its core, uncertainty really is all about fear. Usually fear of the present and the future, but sometimes the past as well if we're lucky. And when we are afraid, our brains change, and we adapt to whatever our circumstances require. We must pay closer attention to ourselves, not less. We need to be checking in on our physical and mental states regularly, sometimes even multiple times a day, in order to ensure that our needs are truly being met. Take a deep breath and ask yourself, *How am I doing? What do I need?* You should be attentive to your pain as much as your needs. If I had taken the time to really take a step back and examine my needs and the extent to which I was performing, I might not have been sick on that street in Greece. I might have been at the hotel and declined the shopping trip. Or at home and not in Greece at all.

Living fully requires us to be honest about what does and does not serve us. I came home from Greece worse than I had been when I left, and I don't want that for you. Actions have consequences. For those of us who are caretakers or responsible for other people, a focus on our own needs can seem indulgent, and even irresponsible. But consider how much harder you are making your situation. Do you want to burn out? Are you ready to get sick or damage your health? In many cases, you wind up hurting yourself to strive for things that no longer fit during this period of pain with an unforeseen ending. So, pause your performance. Cancel it for good...or at least for some time so it doesn't damage you.

When we are in a state of fight-or-flight, whether we realize it or not, our bodies do what they need to do to protect us. Human beings generally have three responses to fear: fight, flight, or freeze. Instead of fighting for my health, I fought for my pride. My desire to be seen a certain way by people—as competent, successful, hardworking, and most importantly, able to bear more than most. But though we are strong, we subdue and overlook our needs in service to our egos. We want it to be for a granular purpose why we perform to a level to damage ourselves. We want to believe it is because our loved one needs us or due to terrible circumstances out of our control. Yet, a lot of times it is merely because we are catering to our biggest love of all: who we think we are, our ego.

All week long as I struggled with sleep and shortness of breath and lost my voice, I continued to insist I was "fine." I maintained all my teaching duties, wrote an op-ed article during breakfast, and worked on this book, which was originally about being a caretaker.

I could not admit how physically sick I was because it was far too terrifying to be *that* sick. According to neurobiology this is known as adaptive pain suppression. My brain subdued the pain signals. Humans have evolved to protect ourselves when we are, in some sense, at risk. This is, neurobiologically, how we survive unimaginable circumstances. Do you remember that hiker they made a movie about? Aron Ralston, who cut off his own arm with a pocketknife to save his life. We are fully capable as humans of numbing our pain when the circumstances call for it, and that's just what I did, in much less dramatic fashion. Please don't let this be you. Cut the performance, pull the curtain, shut the door. Just stop before you hurt yourself.

When life begins to shift, to change, to rumble and crumble beneath our feet, when we lose clarity and find ourselves in the land of uncertainty, we must let go of control and reckon with the unknown. Acknowledge that you don't know what to do next, that you are unclear, and if it's terrifying, admit that. Tell your loved ones and community what the heck is going on. That you will not be able to sustain this role for the time being. That you must shift with the current that has besieged you. That you must spend time facing whatever you are afraid of.

Some people will understand. They may even help take some of the responsibility off your plate. But you won't know until you address it.

Ignore the signals that you should continue with the status quo. Some people will not be helpful and complain about your need to center yourself. They may even be mad at you. No one else will be there to pick up the pieces. Words to make you feel guilty will be in exchange for your vulnerability. You may be judged wrongfully. The circumstances may fall apart, and other routes will be created to cover for you. All of this may not make you feel good about a decision to center yourself. But you have to face what you're dealing with, no matter how scary, and navigate from that place. Take off your mask so you can move as unencumbered as possible.

That night in Greece, I was admitted to the doctor and learned that my larynx was over 70 percent blocked, which is why I was unable to breathe effectively. I needed to surrender to it. I was winded walking around. The steps from my hotel room to where I taught every day were the equivalent of two to three city blocks, and it made me feel like I had just done a thirty-minute Peloton ride. My lungs were on fire.

I was stuck on the other side of the world, sick and without my family. Being that far away from Matt and Bennett in a foreign clinic, in a country where I don't speak the language, was devastating. Thankfully, the doctor said that yes, it was safe to fly.

The next day I stepped into the sparkling, crystal-clear water and wept. I let the ocean buoy me. I sat with my breath and let the waves pull me. Acceptance shining like the sun on top of me. I did what I came to do, and less than I wanted. And now it was time to stop, unmask, leave…and I wish for you to do the same.

11

...Heal

WEAKNESSES WILL SHOW themselves. When the ground beneath your feet starts to quake, and the road ahead looks bleak, that's when insecurities and pain points will rise to the surface to say hello. You've been hiding from them, running emotional and mental races to avoid seeing them, sometimes without even realizing it, but during your most challenging times, they will start to gather in the fog. These past traumas that you haven't fully processed, the things that still cause you anxiety quietly, will rise to the surface during moments of pain, and you will be forced to reckon with them.

This is obviously unfair. Aren't you already dealing with enough? Working mom, overscheduled kids, and sick parents feels like more than enough, and now while enrolling your mother into an assisted-living facility, you're also encountering complicated feelings about your childhood relationship with her that increase your feelings of anxiety and emotional depletion. You didn't have that on your bingo card for this year. The last thing you want to do when you're experiencing uncertainty is deal with complex emotions from the past, but I can promise they are coming for you. Stress, unfortunately, brings them to the surface quickly.

In the midst of overwhelming stress, we are more sensitive emotionally because our systems are overwhelmed. Our brains are forced to process, in many cases, more than they can practically handle and we are like a living, breathing, open wound. I want you to think of yourself, when navigating uncertainty, like a small child at 4:00 p.m. on the brink of losing your shit after you've been on the playground and in the classroom learning all day. You are headed for a meltdown at any moment and the things you will find most triggering are the triggers you haven't fully figured out how to manage. The things you've buried way down deep and don't even dare to think about, but when stress levels rise and you are more mentally, emotionally, and physically overwhelmed, they will appear out of nowhere.

You can try to ignore them, swallow them, stuff them down, or you can use them to facilitate deeper healing.

In my case, long COVID made me into the thing I have feared the most since childhood: a sick mom. I was afraid of becoming a sick mom because I'd had one. I would rather be almost anything than a sick mom. As much as I didn't want to be a sick person, there is something about the idea of being a sick mother that breaks me. It breaks me because I know just how hard it can be to be the child of a sick parent.

When I was thirteen, my parents went to New York City for their anniversary. A few days later my mother was sick and could barely get out of bed. She went from being a full-time employee at IBM, Sunday school teacher, PTA leader and school board agitator, Jazzercise aficionado, generally amazing and wonderful mother to two annoying kids, to being bedridden and disabled in what felt like five minutes. Healthy in October, sick in November, officially out of work and on disability by February and no one could tell us what was wrong with her. We didn't know if she would live or die, and at age thirteen, the idea of life without my mother was unbearable.

We shuttled her to doctors and specialists nonstop for nearly four years seeking solutions. She spent time in and out of hospitals, and she learned how to get around pretty effectively with a cane or motorized wheelchair. At thirteen I took on more responsibilities at home: laundry, grocery shopping, cooking, cleaning, and the like, and we all did whatever we had to do to survive. Ultimately, four years later, when I was seventeen and she was just forty-one, doctors identified lesions on her brain. She had multiple sclerosis, and we were told that the disease had done permanent and irreparable damage to her brain. I will never forget those words "permanent and irreparable," so painfully clear and final and almost poetic. Those words were also sadly validating. For years, she had been mostly ignored and dismissed by doctors and specialists up and down and around New York State. She was a lower-middle class uneducated Black woman and almost no one listened to her. You would sit with doctors, befuddled by this very sick woman in front of them and unable to solve the problem, and you could feel them wondering, *Perhaps this is all just in her head?* Indeed, it was, just not in the ways her doctors ever suspected.

As a teenager, to watch your parent go from healthy to having some degree of brain damage in the span of just a few years is horrifying. The experience of her illness and diagnosis is nearly twenty years old and I still get sweaty palms when I talk about it. The suddenness combined with the injustice of it all is too much pain for me to bear as her child. The woman has been dead for eighteen years, and I still find myself enraged by it all.

A few years ago, I was attending a work dinner that included some pharmaceutical executives and one of them works on MS for a major Fortune 500 drug manufacturer. When I told her my mother spent four years seeking answers and trying to secure a diagnosis for her MS, she said, "I am so sorry, and this is horrible to say, but for our minority patients that's actually pretty remarkable. The average is seven to ten years from initial symptoms to diagnosis." Seven to ten years of suffering primarily for being born the wrong color is disgusting. I drowned my horror in boulevardiers that night. And this is what I mean about hiding. I can talk about my mother's illness from a distance. I can discuss it in bullet points and use her story to give speeches and raise money to help similarly affected men and women, but when it comes to the actual feelings of the thing, I prefer bourbon.

So when I first found myself sick, unable to consider that I was about to enter into similar territory as my mom—an unknown illness, with no real known cause or cure or set timelines or treatment regimen, that I might just have to learn to live with—this thing that kept me from being able to even cook bacon properly, was unfathomable. I refused to accept it and spent months looking for any answer to my pain that wasn't long COVID. I didn't want a repeat of her experience. My spirit couldn't handle that. I shuttled myself to my own bevy of specialists seeking anything else that could be wrong with my body.

Perhaps it was a hormonal imbalance, or maybe a really bad sinus infection, maybe I even needed sinus surgery. I wanted to know that whatever was happening to my body could be easily repaired.

It all felt too familiar, and I couldn't face the fact that I was living a similar story to hers. The way her disease swooped in and caught us all unaware and then completely consumed our lives and altered our family is an experience I don't think I will ever really recover from, so when I felt it happening to me, instead of owning it and finding a way to live my own story, I downplayed the seriousness of it all. I figured if I could just get my headaches under control I would be fine. I focused on symptom management as opposed to a whole-body approach to my health. *It's just a headache*, I told myself over and over again because that was so much easier than admitting that I had this big, scary, uncontrollable thing that would eventually take my health, my mental well-being, and a whole lot of money along with it. I refused to face my reality and ultimately that caused more suffering. It delayed my treatments, impaired my ability to ask for help, and added underlying stress and anxiety that I absolutely did not need.

This is what happens when we refuse to acknowledge our pain: We cause more suffering. We know this. Pain points us to a problem, that is the purpose of it, but when we ignore the pain, we ignore the problem, and we don't heal. My mother's illness, death, and the resulting impact on our family does not necessarily make me depressed or even sad, but it still hurts, it stings in the way that a paper cut does during normal times. However, during hard times, it feels like a heart attack. It is tremendous and uncomfortable and can trigger a full-on internal freak-out, that I've learned to mask. When we first brought Bennett home, it was a time of joy and the stress of being a new parent, and after seventy-two hours of no sleep, I cried like a baby myself wishing my mother was here. And we all have these experiences in life that shape us, live on in us, and show up when life is at its worst.

Whether it's the hurtful feeling of a past relationship or experience that left you crushed, the pain, grief, and trauma we overcome still live on in us and when uncertainty arises, if we want to live well in the midst of it, we must deepen our awareness of these things to ensure the past doesn't impede our current healing.

I didn't want to do it, but I knew I had a lot of hard work to do to separate my story from my mother's. I needed to change the narrative. To recognize that what happened to her isn't exactly what is happening to me. I have never been to an AA or NA meeting, but there is a reason for the meetings and the notion that you are always in recovery. I have a friend who has been in recovery for nearly twenty years, and he celebrates his sobriety each year and actively speaks about being "in recovery" in the present tense, all these years later. He still acknowledges there is something he personally has to continue to work on and heal. It is lifelong work.

We should assume the same for all forms of deep emotional and psychological pain. The painful experiences that form us don't just disappear; they remain a part of our psyche and can continue to cause pain if we don't acknowledge and find ways to cope with them. You know exactly what I mean. There are these things that people can say or do to us, or things that happen to us today that make us feel angry, sad, or scared because of something that happened in our past. When something hits you and makes you feel bad, you need to first acknowledge it, because sometimes acknowledging it may be more than enough.

After returning from Greece, still barely able to breathe, I had a Zoom call with a friend. She asked me, "Do you want to be here?" At first, I didn't even really understand the question. What was she suggesting? That I might actually jump off a bridge or something? God no. I understand suicide and suicidal ideation because, sadly, I have been there before. This was not that, but she did hit on something.

"No. Not like this," I said.

I had to either choose avoidance again or put down all distractions—bourbon included—and acknowledge my trauma and commit to my healing. I had to admit

I was carrying too much and that led me to a place where I didn't want my life. I did not want to live. It wasn't that I wanted to end my life, but I didn't want to live *how* I had to now. To carry on with so much physical and emotional pain. I didn't know how to do it, so I wanted it all to just stop. I wanted to be done.

As soon as I admitted that I felt a shift. Not in a seismic way, but in a gentle way, like water lapping at the shore of a lake; I could feel the simple admittance create an opening. I suddenly felt capable and motivated. I was going to do whatever I needed to do to heal. I felt stronger—not physically, but emotionally. I uncovered a sense of resolve, a commitment. When we force ourselves to acknowledge our pain, it often feels like weakness, when in reality it is strength. Strength comes, in part, from knowing yourself fully. When you know who you are, how you came to be, what hurts you, and what makes you happy, you are more fully equipped to move through the world when life is hard and when it isn't. In that deeply uncomfortable moment, I committed to my healing, to using this horrible illness as an opportunity to transform into someone even more healthy, happy, and whole than I was before.

After that admission, I cried and cried and cried, and tears are important, but healing is also about action. Therapy on its own isn't a decisive enough action. Healing is work. In my case, I decided I was going to start by making a list.

I love lists. I started a list on my phone called "The 100." I decided I would hold myself accountable to my healing by tracking every decision I made that prioritized me and my physical and emotional well-being above all else, until I had one hundred items. That felt like the right amount for me to trick my brain into behaving differently over the long-term. I needed to learn how to prioritize myself. I was clearly struggling and needed to really focus with intention on my physical and mental health. I needed to change my life, how I behaved, how I treated myself, how I treated others. I needed to focus on Marisa. It was not optional but necessary if I was going to survive this period of illness that had been going on for over a year. I want you to figure out what the work looks like for you. For me, it was taking on my trauma with a list to confront it. I needed to develop my own version of accountability, and since I am a girl who loves a good list, I went with that, but that may not be what's best for you. Take the time to figure out what the work looks like for you and do it.

The hard things that happen to us in this life change our ability to deal with the next hard thing because even when we move past our challenges, we never forget about them. And when uncertainty arises and life becomes stressful and overwhelming, we must put down the things that don't serve us, and avoiding your pain does not serve you, it slows you down.

This is how we all must move through the world. We are each a collection of our lived experiences. As much as we may want the past to simply stay in the past, our past is what forms us and it is what informs our stories about us. Good and bad, the things we have lived through are a part of us and the things that cause us pain should change how we engage with and interact with the world—they have to. They change us and then we get to decide what to do with ourselves. Do we continue to try to avoid the hard stuff, or do we lean all the way in and use the hard things to facilitate further healing? At the end of the day healing isn't about overcoming, but about integrating.

In the case of my mom's illness, I simply hadn't truly integrated it into my life. The trauma of that formative experience was so large, I did not want to deal with it, and the further I got from it the sillier it felt to even have to deal with it at all. The thing that needs to be dealt with is often the thing you don't want to think about, the thing you don't want to admit.

I didn't want to deal with recognizing all the pain and suffering my perfect mom, sweet Lisa, had to endure. I don't want to deal with or think about how hard her illness made our life. It makes me feel guilty thinking about it because that makes her illness about me, but what about her? What about her dreams? What about her physical pain? Her mental anguish? The grief she must have felt going from fully able to disabled? What about that? The questions and the heartache that lingers beneath the surface, those are the things you must contend with in order to heal and make it through life's challenges and uncertainties. That grief is real, no matter how old it is. We all want to avoid dealing with hard things, but avoidance only increases stress and leaves us more prone to depression.

So when uncertainty arises in your life, ask yourself, *What else about me and my life is going to make this harder, or more painful?* To live well, confronting and healing our wounds, is a daily practice, not a one and done. There will be good days, where you feel like, *Oh I can do anything I put my mind to! I am going to be OK! This really isn't so bad! I can even make bacon again!* And on bad days, the goal is to pull yourself out of a storyline rooted in your past, not your present.

12

Hope...

Hope is the only thing that really matters in this world, it is the only thing that has ever produced anything of use to us. Hope holds the power to change the world, and eventually your circumstances as well. Hope is a disciplined practice. It is not light or cheerful or a synonym for optimism. It is the energy that drives us forward when life feels impossible. Whether it is developed through your faith, spirituality, or love, hope is the fuel that keeps you moving forward toward a better future. Love is what gets you through; hope is what pushes you forward. Hope provides stability. When times are hard, it is innate in us as human beings to reach for hope.

The current popular definition of hope is, "a feeling of expectation and desire for a certain thing to happen." But I prefer the archaic definition of hope, "a feeling of trust."

The hope we seek must be rooted in our current reality. If you're going through a financial struggle, hoping to win the lotto is frivolous and frankly stupid. The odds are never in your favor. Hope is trusting something better is coming your way, and then doing whatever is necessary to make it so. My hope, and my commitment to hope, is ruthless.

When life gets hard at times, we often want to give up, to give in to defeat and despair. We despise our current reality, we don't know what to do, and we just want it to be over. We ask, *Why have I been forced into this and how do I get out? When will it be over?* One day, when I realized I'd been sick for over a year and still was nowhere near "normal," Matt found me curled up in a ball on the floor of my office, bawling. I am talking about the kind of ugly cry where you can't catch your breath, you're not making any sense, and you're just choking on snot and tears. Not a pretty sight. The isolation and pain of illness, coupled with the pressure I felt to get better and make things right again, plus the work of motherhood and running a business—it was all just too much and I broke.

Let yourself break. Tears water the seeds of growth and transformation. There is nothing bad about an ugly cry. Mourn what feels lost. Sleep it off and commit again to hope.

You don't need to feel hope every second of every day, because that is not realistic, but the more you practice, the bigger your muscle for it will get when you are faced with despair. Hope allows you to be in pain but still have the mental and spiritual space to take action. Your problems are real, and they are things that require bigger solutions than simply a mindset shift. If I could meditate my way out of illness, or just "think positive" when overwhelmed with sadness, that would be great, but that's not how it works. The stress you feel is real and shouldn't be minimalized by some wellness guru. Hope is serious business; it can allow you to take the steps you need to make the big decisions that living with uncertainty requires.

In the 1940s, my grandfather, my Pop-Pop, a man with just a seventh-grade education, was a hard worker and a leader in the fields where he worked down South in Statesboro, Georgia. The South was home. The red clay of Georgia runs through our veins and is built into our DNA, but home had become too dangerous. He believed in his heart that staying down South was not the right decision, nor the safest one, for his family so he decided to leave Georgia for a new opportunity in Florida, with the ultimate goal being a move North.

The night before they were set to leave Georgia, the white man who owned the fields where my Pop-Pop worked and a few of his buddies showed up at my grandparents' home with trace chains. I had to google what these were when my aunt told me that. I learned that they are the thick metal chains used to attach a horse to a wagon. Their intent was clear: beat him into submission and force him to stay and work for them. My grandfather met them at his front door, shotgun in hand. The men left, and the next day my grandparents, uncles, and aunt left Georgia. A few months later, his opportunity to move "up North" arrived in the form of a man from the Hudson Valley with a job offer. My family became a part of the six million Black Americans who fled the blatant racial terror and constant violence of the South, for the quiet and more subtle racism of the North during the Great Migration.

If not for my grandfather's commitment to hope, his trust that something better must exist for him and for his family, and his willingness to do anything he needed to make that future a reality, I would not be here. I am confident that my education, my books, my economic stability and mobility, my physical and emotional safety today are derived from his hope and his shotgun. A shotgun raised in the dark that saved generations. He knew there had to be something better and he made a commitment to finding it by any means necessary.

My grandfather's courage and what my family has previously endured in this country make me less afraid. This is why I remain ruthlessly committed to hope and healing. My family, and I'm sure yours as well, has survived more than what we are living through during this time of global instability. In many cases our ancestors have all known racism, sexism, religious and political persecution, and war, and the family survived. You are proof of their enduring hope. In the midst of uncertainty, draw on that well of inherited hope when you run out of your own.

I often think of this quote from the Bible that I think works whether you're religious or not: "Hope that is seen is no hope at all. For who hopes for what he already has?" Hope requires you to sit in a space of darkness and reach for the light. It pushes you to wait for dawn. Instead of hoping for a miracle, all I choose to hope for is clarity, a sense of direction, a lit match to briefly navigate the darkness. Hope is your guide to life's next chapter.

To push through the fog of uncertainty, to place our trust in something better while being honest about our current circumstances, whatever they may be, is how we survive whole. We must remove hope out of an idealistic, pie-in-the-sky, social-media-hashtag framework, and use it for what it is really meant for: to move us forward, sometimes mere inches at a time, to a slightly better place.

Shifts may be subtle, progress minimal, but hope is continual. It is only in looking back that we can see the enormity of our hope and all that it has done over time.

Hope is a bridge between where you sit today and where you want to go. Life circumstances are not always linear; twists and turns, going up and back down, occur. So as you sit with your darkness, with whatever painful event or set of circumstances has turned your life upside down, remember to cling to hope, because no matter how dark the night, hope can always light your way.

Acknowledgments

The week this book was due, I lost my grandmother, Lossie Mae Lee, at nearly 102 years old. She had this saying she used often that I think is fitting here: "Don't forget the bridge that brought you across." I wrote this book during a deeply challenging time for me and my family. I needed a very big bridge so there are a lot of people to thank.

First and foremost, the simple fact that you are holding this book is a testament to God's grace, and the power of deep community and mutual aid.

Most importantly, Matthew, this book is for you. Unfortunately, you know more about navigating uncertainty than most people and there is no one in the world I'd rather wait for dawn alongside. I wish we were called to do so less frequently, but when uncertainty arises, I think we bear it pretty well

ACKNOWLEDGMENTS

together. You are everything to me and I am so glad you are Bennett's dad.

To my son, Bennett, it is a blessing to be your mother. I love you to infinity and beyond. You are my joy. And to everyone who helped care for you while I was sick and writing this book, I owe a huge debt of gratitude, most of all to your amazing nanny, Miss Julianna Runza. Julianna, I love you and this book probably would not exist without you. Also, to the entire Runza-Antonakos family, who kept me well fed physically and emotionally, thank you. You all brought so much joy and light into such a dark year: Carmella, Greg, Bennett's besties Mila and Cora, and their wonderful grandparents, too. You all made this year less lonely and far more fun than it would have been without you.

To the people who help me create books and make sure you buy them, I obviously could not do this without you. Primarily, to my editor, dear friend, and chief encouragement officer, Krishan Trotman: You are brilliant and kind, and I am so thankful we found our way to each other. I do believe our moms had something to do with that! To the rest of the Hachette/Legacy Lit/Grand Central Publishing family, including but not limited to Amina Iro, Mahito Indi Henderson, Estefania Acquaviva, and Maya Lewis, thanks so much for all you do! To my agent, Marya Spence, thank you for taking me on during your own period

ACKNOWLEDGMENTS

of uncertainty. I think it's worked out pretty well for both of us! Extra special thanks to my publicity team, led by Jackson Musker and my cousin Jessica Lee. I couldn't sell this book without you.

Dr. Christy Denckla, the best friend and research adviser a girl could ask for, I could not have done this without you. Thank you for always being flexible with my crazy schedule and for making me sound much smarter than I am! Liza Fitzpatrick, thank you for being my first reader. Your kind and critical feedback definitely made this a better book. Allison Brownell Salzer, you stepped in to make sure I had the personal and professional support I needed when I was too sick to even speak most days. I am so thankful our not-so-great basketball skills brought us together. To Viv, Quinn, and Dave, thanks for sharing her with me.

To my father Sam for showing me how to have fun and letting me write whatever I want about him. To my sister Heather, for being an example of resilience and courage in the face of adversity. Bennett is so lucky to have you both and Uncle Jamane too!

To our big extended family, especially my Aunt Clarine and my late grandparents, Sam and Lossie Lee, who are my ever-present reminder to keep hoping and moving forward, my cousin Courtney Amal, and to my godparents, Tim and Andrea, thank you.

ACKNOWLEDGMENTS

To all the friends and mentors without whom I know I wouldn't be as happy or successful or content as I am today. They are the people who show up over and over again for me personally and professionally, and I would be lost without them. They write blurbs, edit social media posts, send cookies, share my work, build my website, make doctors' appointments, hire me for projects, and always make me laugh: Subrina and Ryan Jendrasiak, Naomi Ages, Alisha Moran, Gloriana Salgado, Bridget Marvinsmith, Seo Yun Yang, Adriana Cosgriff, Vivian Bertseka Lemmer, Falyne Chave, Elizabeth Cleary, Danae Pauli, Scott, Megan, JJ, and Jacob Quimby, Dan and Nicole Curran, Reshma Saujani, Emily Oster, Emily Tisch Sussman, Chris Cormier Magianno, Anthony Hayes, Maggie Smith, Alexa Lynch, Michelle Hord, Lisa Keefauver, Brian Wallach, Sandra Abrevaya, Claire Bidwell Smith, Elizabeth Holmes, Glennon Doyle, Andrea James, Chloe Cockburn, Zack Carpenter, Mollie Chen, Alicia Menendez, Kwame Owusu-Kesse, Jazmine Lewis, Michael Hill, Deesha Dyer, Kiese Laymon, Adam Grant, Tembi Locke, Willie and Christina Geist, Katie Murphy, Rachel Fulginiti, and anyone else who has helped me be able to put words on paper this year, thank you so much for your invaluable help.

To the team at Rosemary's House and the women who supported me when I got sick abroad, your gentleness and care changed me and how I move in the

ACKNOWLEDGMENTS

world. I cannot thank you enough for your love: Angelica Rose Toumbas, Eunhye Oak, and Crystal Dalton.

My new friend and long COVID sherpa, Anna Makatche, I don't know what I would have done without your insights, advice, support, and encouragement this year. Navigating this illness alongside you was so much easier than doing it all alone. To Rebecca Cokley and the Disability Justice team at the Ford Foundation, thank you for reading this book, for believing in me, and for supporting my efforts to help those navigating disability as a result of long COVID. To Dr. Robert Ross and the team at the California Endowment, thank you for your financial support of my work at the intersection of racism and grief.

To every doctor, nurse, therapist, and assistant who has helped me navigate life with long COVID, thank you. Special thanks to Dr. Lee Coleman Hinnant, Dr. Christie Garb, Dr. Gillian Goddard, Dr. Hida Nierenburg, Erika Forsell, LAc, Justin Feldman, and Emily Boland.

To everyone who sent a kind word, care package, thoughtful text, funny meme, and to all the folks named in this book, thank you for inspiring and supporting me. A special thank-you to the greatest dog that ever lived, our sweet Sadie girl. She sat beside us in every season of uncertainty, and our hearts have been forever changed by her love.

ACKNOWLEDGMENTS

    Lastly, to my readers, thank you. I keep a note on my bulletin board when I'm writing books, "Remember who you write for." I write for you. May these words help you or someone you love to heal.

With gratitude, hope, and love,

Marisa

Bibliography

Amit, Z., Galina, Z. H. (1986). "Stress-induced analgesia: Adaptive pain suppression." *Physiological Reviews* 66 (4), 1091–1120.

Barlow, Jameta Nicole. "Black Women, the Forgotten Survivors of Sexual Assault." *American Psychological Association.* (February 1, 2020). https://www.apa.org/topics/sexual-assault-harassment/black-women-sexual-violence.

Berkman, L. F. and Glass, T. (2000). "Social integration, social networks, social support, and health." *Social Epidemiology* 1(6), 137–173.

Bonanno, G. A. et al. (1995). "When avoiding unpleasant emotions might not be such a bad thing: Verbal-autonomic response dissociation and midlife conjugal bereavement." *Journal of Personality and Social Psychology* 69(5), 975–989.

Bonanno, G. A., Shuquan C., Galatzer-Levy, I. R. (2023). "Resilience to potential trauma and adversity through regulatory flexibility." *Nature Reviews Psychology* 2 (11), 663–675.

Butler, R. K., Finn, D. P. (2009). "Stress-induced analgesia." *Progress in Neurobiology* 88 (3) 184–202.

BIBLIOGRAPHY

Cacioppo, S., Capitanio, J. P., and Cacioppo, J. T. (2014). "Toward a neurology of loneliness." *Psychological Bulletin* 140(6), 1464.

Carola, V., et al. (2024). "Psychological risk factors and cardiovascular disease." *Frontiers in Psychology* 15, 1419731.

Carstensen, L. L. (2021). "Socioemotional selectivity theory: The role of perceived endings in human motivation." *The Gerontologist* 61(8) 1188–1196.

Cohen, S. (2021). "Psychosocial vulnerabilities to upper respiratory infectious illness: Implications for susceptibility to Coronavirus disease 2019 (COVID-19)." *Perspectives on Psychological Science* 16(1), 161–174.

Collins, N. L., Ford, M. B. (2010). "Responding to the needs of others: The caregiving behavioral system in intimate relationships." *Journal of Social and Personal Relationships* 27 (2) 235-244.

Cross, C. J., Fomby, P., and Letiecq, B. (2022). "Interlinking structural racism and heteropatriarchy: Rethinking family structure's effects on child outcomes in a racialized, unequal society." *Journal of Family Theory & Review* 14(3), 482–501.

Denckla, C. A., et al. (2020). "Psychological resilience: An update on definitions, a critical appraisal, and research recommendations." *European Journal of Psychotraumatology* 11(1), 1822064.

Dimidjian, S., et al. (2011). "The origins and current status of behavioral activation treatments for depression." *Annual Review of Clinical Psychology* 7(1), 1–38.

Farr, A. M., Carter, J. S., and Webber-Ritchey, K. J. (2025). "Relationships among endorsement of the Superwoman Schema and health outcomes." *Journal of Obstetric, Gynecologic & Neonatal Nursing* 54(1), 88–101.

Gottman, J., Silver, N. (2015). *The Seven Principles for Making Marriage Work: A Practical Guide from the Country's Foremost Relationship Expert.* Harmony, New York.

BIBLIOGRAPHY

Goubert, L., and Trompetter, H. (2017). "Towards a science and practice of resilience in the face of pain." *European Journal of Pain* 21(8), 1301–1315.

Hikichi, H., et al. (2017). "Social capital and cognitive decline in the aftermath of a natural disaster: A natural experiment from the 2011 Great East Japan Earthquake and Tsunami." *The Lancet Planetary Health* 1(3), e105–e113.

Hofmann, S. G., Asmundson, G. J. G., and Beck, A.T. (2013). "The science of cognitive therapy." *Behavior Therapy* 44 (2) 199–212.

Holinger, Dorothy P. (2020). *The Anatomy of Grief.* Yale University Press.

Infurna, F. J., and Mayer, A. (2019). "Repeated bereavement takes its toll on subjective well-being." *Innovation in Aging* 3(4) igz047.

Janoff-Bulman, R., et al. (1987). "Coping with traumatic life events: The role of denial in light of people's assumptive worlds." In C. R. Snyder and C. E. Ford eds. *Coping with Negative Life Events: Clinical and Social Psychological Perspectives.* Plenum Press, New York.

Kalisch, R., Russo, S. J., and Müller, M. B. (2024). "Neurobiology and systems biology of stress resilience." *Physiological Reviews* 104(3), 1205–1263.

Karam, E.G., et al. (2014). "Cumulative traumas and risk thresholds: 12-month PTSD in the World Mental Health (WMH) surveys." *Depression and Anxiety* 31(2), 130–142.

Kenkel, W. M., Perkeybile, A. M., and Carter, C. S. (2017). "The neurobiological causes and effects of alloparenting." *Developmental Neurobiology* 77(2), 214–232.

Kross, E., and Ayduk, O. (2017). "Self-distancing: Theory, research, and current directions." *Advances in Experimental Social Psychology* (vol. 55, pp. 81–136). Academic Press.

Lam, J. A., et al. (2021). "Neurobiology of loneliness: a systematic review." *Neuropsychopharmacology* 46(11), 1873–1887.

Lazarus, R. S., and Folkman, S. (1984). *Stress, Appraisal, and Coping.* Springer Publishing.

Lee, S., Colditz, G. A., Berkman, L. F., and Kawachi, I. (2003). "Caregiving and risk of coronary heart disease in US women: A prospective study." *American Journal of Preventive Medicine* 24(2), 113–119.

Lewis, T. T., Cogburn, C. D., Williams, D. R. (2015). "Self-reported experiences of discrimination and health: Scientific advances, ongoing controversies, and emerging issues." *Annual Review of Clinical Psychology* 11(1) 407–440.

McEwen, B. S. (1998). "Stress, adaptation, and disease: Allostasis and allostatic load." *Annals of the New York Academy of Sciences* 840(1), 33–44.

McEwen, Bruce S. (2013). "The brain on stress: Toward an integrative approach to brain, body, and behavior." *Perspectives on Psychological Science* 8 (6) 673–675.

Mikulincer, M. and Shaver, P. R. (2023). *Attachment Theory Expanded.* Guilford Publications.

Moseley, G. L., and Butler, D. S. (2015). "Fifteen years of explaining pain: The past, present, and future." *Journal of Pain* 16(9), 807–813.

O'Connor, M. F. (2022). *The Grieving Brain: The Surprising Science of How We Learn from Love and Loss.* HarperCollins: New York.

O'Connor, M. F. (2025) *The Grieving Body: How the Stress of Loss Can Be an Opportunity for Healing.* HarperOne: New York.

Office of the Surgeon General (OSG). (2023). "Our epidemic of loneliness and isolation: The U.S. Surgeon General's Advisory on the healing effects of social connection and community." Washington (DC): US Department of Health and Human Services.

BIBLIOGRAPHY

Ong, A. D., Uchino, B. N., and Wethington, E. (2016). "Loneliness and health in older adults: A mini-review and synthesis." *Gerontology* 62(4), 443–449.

Ploghaus, A., et al. (2001). "Exacerbation of pain by anxiety is associated with activity in a hippocampal network." *Journal of Neuroscience* 21(24), 9896–9903.

Pluess, M., and Belsky, J. (2009). "Differential susceptibility to rearing experience: The case of childcare." *Journal of Child Psychology and Psychiatry* 50(4), 396–404.

Schornick, Z., et al. (2023). "Hope that benefits others: A systematic literature review of hope theory and prosocial outcomes." *International Journal of Applied Positive Psychology* 8(1), 37–61.

Schut, M. S. H. (1999). "The dual process model of coping with bereavement: Rationale and description." *Death Studies* 23(3), 197–224.

Shear, K., et al. (2007). "An attachment-based model of complicated grief including the role of avoidance." *European Archives of Psychiatry and Clinical Neuroscience* 257, 453–461.

Snyder, C. R. (2002). "Hope theory: Rainbows in the mind." *Psychological Inquiry* 13(4), 249–275.

Szewczyk, W., et al. (2024). "Long COVID and recovery from Long COVID: Quality of life impairments and subjective cognitive decline at a median of 2 years after initial infection." *BMC Infectious Diseases* 24(1), 1–13.

UN Doc. CERD/C/USA/CO/7-9. (September 2014). "Concluding Observations of the Committee on the Elimination of Racial Discrimination, United States of America." https://hrlibrary.umn.edu/country/usa2014.html.

Woods-Giscombé, C. L. (2010). "Superwoman schema: African American women's views on stress, strength, and health." *Qualitative Health Research* 20(5), 668–683.

ALSO AVAILABLE